IN THE LIGHT OF
humane nature

IN THE LIGHT OF
humane nature

HUMAN VALUES, NATURE, THE GREEN ECONOMY, AND ENVIRONMENTAL SALVATION

ARTHUR B. WEISSMAN

NEW YORK

IN THE LIGHT OF humane nature
Human Values, Nature, the Green Economy, and Environmental Salvation

Published in New York, New York, by Morgan James Publishing. Morgan James and The Entrepreneurial Publisher are trademarks of Morgan James, LLC. www.MorganJamesPublishing.com

The Morgan James Speakers Group can bring authors to your live event. For more information or to book an event visit The Morgan James Speakers Group at www.TheMorganJamesSpeakersGroup.com.

For information on the sustainability of the paper used in this book, please see: http://www1.lightningsource.com/chainofcustody/.

FREE eBook edition for your existing eReader with purchase

PRINT NAME ABOVE

For more information, instructions, restrictions, and to register your copy, go to **www.bitlit.ca/readers/register** or use your QR Reader to scan the barcode:

ISBN 978-1-61448-760-9 paperback
ISBN 978-1-61448-761-6 eBook
ISBN 978-1-61448-762-3 audio
ISBN 978-1-61448-864-4 hard cover
Library of Congress Control Number: 2013945577

Cover Design by:
Rachel Lopez
www.r2cdesign.com

Interior Design by:
Bonnie Bushman
bonnie@caboodlegraphics.com

In an effort to support local communities, raise awareness and funds, Morgan James Publishing donates a percentage of all book sales for the life of each book to Habitat for Humanity Peninsula and Greater Williamsburg.

Get involved today, visit
www.MorganJamesBuilds.com.

Habitat for Humanity®
Peninsula and Greater Williamsburg
Building Partner

To Hope Phyllis Weissman
(1944-2002)

Table of Contents

Table of Contents

Preface

....

The seeds for this work were sown both recently and long ago.
While wading through Los Angeles traffic several years ago as we
went from interview to interview, Barbara Hodgson, Green Seal's
publicist, and I rambled through many topics, including what
is conventionally known as environmental ethics. I mentioned
that I had written a kind of master's thesis years before about the
topic,[1] and I briefly described its main themes. From that time
on, Barbara encouraged me to resurrect and publish the work to
explain what I do as the head of Green Seal, the non-profit US
environmental certification organization.

I finally dug out the thesis and reread it. Familiar phrases,
passages, and concepts alternated with mostly forgotten
arguments. I realized that, whatever its merits, the thesis

---

1   *Nature and Human Values*, unpublished, 1975.

deserved to be left in peace, while the themes within it might still have value in the updated context of my professional and personal experiences, as well as global environmental and social developments, since I wrote it. To carry forth those themes, I abstracted key passages from the thesis, a few of which appear in this work as epigraphs.[2]

I thank Barbara Hodgson for her gentle persistence and faith in my work. She is the godmother of this book.

I also took heart that those themes were worth adapting by the profoundly thoughtful and personal comments of my major advisor on the master's thesis, the late Joseph A. Miller of the Yale School of Forestry and Environmental Studies. Joe was an historian and librarian *par excellence*, and he did both with quiet zeal.

Of course, my intention in writing this book goes far beyond reviving concepts from my past. Increasingly over my career, as environmental problems have multiplied in gravity and scope, I have wondered what it will take for human beings to appreciate the world around them and the jeopardy they are putting it in. Even as our economy has grown modestly greener and sustainability has become a watchword in business the past twenty years, the overall environmental health of our planet continues to decline. Companies may parade their sustainability reports and awards, but tropical deforestation, habitat and species loss, pervasive toxic pollution, and disruptive climate change continue at dangerous levels, some at accelerated rates. No matter what we have done so far, we hit a wall on reversing our disastrous course. This book puts forth an underlying reason for our environmental crisis and poses a solution to it.

---

2   Specifically, the epigraphs in the middle of chapter 1 and at the beginning of chapter 5.

This is not to say that the work of Green Seal and others in protecting the environment and making the economy more sustainable has been in vain. To the contrary: our environmental and health conditions would be far worse today without such efforts, and they have provided clear guidance on the way our economy needs to change and business and society need to operate to ensure a more sustainable future. As "the original Green Seal of approval," Green Seal has developed environmental leadership standards for dozens of product and service categories and has certified thousands of products and services that meet the standards. Green Seal has also worked with many government and private agencies to make their operations (purchasing, facilities, etc.) more environmentally responsible, and it has produced numerous guidances in this vein for sectors ranging from office buildings to campuses to hotels and restaurants.

I have been fortunate to be part of the nascent green economy movement for more than twenty years, having joined Green Seal in 1993 and led it since 1996 as it evolved from a theoretical concept to a market force. In addition to overseeing and directing Green Seal's programs and activities over this period, I have participated in both national and international efforts to disseminate green practices through standards, guidances, policies, and laws. The narrative material in chapter 2 draws from this experience, as does the discussion of responsibility for green practices in chapter 3 and of consumer concerns in chapter 4.

Some early readers have questioned my use in the book of generic names for places and companies. I admit that I am not consistent in this regard, but I have been guided by instinct as to when a more specific name would be useful and when it would distract from the narrative or ideas presented. For this work is not about a particular place, company, or person, but about a societal movement, on the one hand, and about human values toward our world and ourselves, on the other. Where I do name people, I have kept to the first person, but the individuals are real. I trust they will not mind the historical references.

While I am disclaiming, I should note that this book does not necessarily represent the views of my organization, Green Seal, except in the shared goal of making the economy and world more sustainable. I nonetheless want to acknowledge the support given by my board of directors in allowing me to write the book as part of my day job. In particular, our chair, Gary Petersen, recognized immediately the book's purpose and fully supported its execution, in keeping with the remarkable support, collegiality, and friendship he has provided over the years. I hope the work will promote Green Seal's mission by garnering attention to the underlying values ultimately required for the market and cultural transformation to sustainability.

I want also to thank my highly capable and committed staff at Green Seal, who have brought the organization to a level of unquestioned credibility. In particular, Green Seal's progress (and continued existence) would not have been possible without two colleagues who have been with me for most of my years at Green Seal, Mehreteab Masho, our CFO, and Mark Petruzzi, our SVP. Green Seal exists in the first place because of the extraordinary vision of its founder, Rena Shulsky David. Credit is also due to the two earlier board chairs who guided us in our formative years, Denis Hayes and Bryan Thomlison.

At the risk of omitting many worthy ones, I would like to mention the following Green Seal clients for their unwavering commitment to the cause and for the collegiality I have personally shared with them over the years: Marvin Klein (PortionPac), Mark Stanland (Wausau Paper), Rocky Massin (Hillyard), George Milner (Mohawk Paper), Rob Kohlhagen (Diversey/Sealed Air), Debbie Lema (Racine Industries), John Burns (Whole Foods), Rich Davis (Georgia-Pacific), Roger Dower (Johnson Foundation at Wingspread), Jeffrey Smith and Jason Luke (Harvard University), Isabelle Faivre (Cascades), Bill Schalitz (Spartan Chemical), Yalmaz Siddiqui (Office Depot), Mike Koenig and Mark Mikkelson (Andersen), Roger McFadden (Staples), Mike Sawchuk (formerly Enviro-Solutions), Dan Rosenthal (The Rosenthal Group), and Kevin Carter (Airlie Center).

The following Green Seal partners have similarly helped our mission and my job immeasurably: Gary Davis, Marion Stecklow, Claire Barnett, Jane Paul, Kit Cole, Jacquie Ottman, Ed Begley Jr., Jeff Glassie, Julie Baylor, Ashok Kamal, Debbie Levin, Bill Daddi, Eloise Karlatiras, Greg DiMedio, Alicia Culver, Scot Case, Jennifer Wright, Steve Ashkin, Anastasia O'Rourke, Ning Yu, Pierre Hauselmann, John Paul Kusz, Steve Peacock, Patti MacJennett, Chito Cajayon, Rochelle Davis, Wendy Gordon, Diane MacEachern, Christine Black, Allen Rathey, Jack Geibig, Amy Spatrisano, and a host of people in government at all levels who would probably prefer to remain anonymous. Finally, Beto Bedolfe of Marisla Foundation has shown unwavering support for and belief in our work for many years.

Going from concept to publication is a journey in itself, and I have several to thank for their critical assistance. Most of all, my executive assistant, Kat Danaher, helped enormously at every stage, from preparing endless variants on proposals to agents and publishers (and keeping me from getting discouraged by the responses) to contributing ideas for the final design and production. She has been a godsend. Speaking of agents, Michael Ebeling, though unable to represent the book, nonetheless gave extensive guidance on finding a suitable publisher and connected us to Morgan James. I cannot thank Michael enough for his professional generosity. Morgan James Publishing has, in turn, provided invaluable assistance in the final production and marketing of the book, as have Linda Chipperfield and Brielle Welzer in Green Seal's marketing and communications department.

My board member, Joanne Fox-Przeworski, spent countless hours reviewing and commenting on the manuscript, going way beyond the call; I, of course, am alone responsible for any remaining errors or stylistic idiosyncrasies Joanne tried valiantly to scrub away. Our strategic consultant, Janet Wikler, also read the manuscript and provided both much appreciated encouragement and also valuable advice from her many years in the publishing industry. My professional editors, Amanda Rooker and Angie Kiesling, provided numerous exceedingly helpful suggestions in their manuscript review, and I am grateful that they understood so well the purpose of the book.

Returning to the roots of this work, I want to thank my friend since college, Tom Paine, for awakening me back then to the aesthetics of landscape architecture, of which he is a master. Likewise, my late first wife, Peggy Bruns, enhanced my appreciation of the built environment through her love for and professional achievements in architectural history and historic preservation. My longtime friend from Connecticut, Jim Pepe, a consummate science teacher and naturalist, encouraged the development of the Green Platform and actually saved a copy of it that enabled its use here. Although my doctoral dissertation does not figure directly here, its concepts run parallel to those in this work; my advisors for the dissertation, the late geomorphologist Reds Wolman and the philosopher Gary Hatfield, helped me hone my thought process and arguments so I could more persuasively write this book. On a more personal note I am grateful to Roy Riddick for being an uncompromising mentor in my fervid adolescence and to Beth Perry for friendship over many years.

I dedicate this work to my late sister, Hope Phyllis Weissman, longtime professor of humanities, medieval studies, and women's studies at the College of Letters at Wesleyan University in Connecticut. Hope fostered my love for literature, the arts, and even sciences early on. While this work may not have met her high standards, I believe she would have approved of its core message (though probably with a wry remark at the unlikelihood of its being realized). Truly, as I wrote in a sonnet for her memorial, "Through all your life you kept your child's heart,/No greater gift to me did you impart."

My parents, Sarah Danzig and Meyer (Mike) Theodore Weissman, encouraged my education over the years, and they set a high standard for professionalism in the social work and medical fields, respectively. My brother has been setting an example and helping me on the way—from the high road, naturally—ever since childhood.

Finally, my current family has long suffered living with this unrepentant environmentalist (and nag, per the beginning of chapter 3). My sons, Joseph and Lowell, may not agree with some of the positions taken here, but I hope the underlying values will be a source of direction and inspiration in the future. My wife, Rebecca, has given so much to the children through the travails of their childhood, and she has postponed her own career even as she has broadened it for the sake of the family by becoming a certified holistic nutritionist (and preparing a book on family health). I deeply appreciate her support over the years as I continued to work at Green Seal. May this book be a wish for a more promising future for our children—and for everyone else's, as well.

Washington, DC
June 2013

CHAPTER 1

Introduction:
And Still the World Burns

··

Flames on the horizon from flare stacks reached like wailing arms into the sky and cast a pall with their unearthly glow. Over time they sputtered, then died, and a Light began glowing in their place. It grew ever stronger and warmer. Plants, animals, and people returned.[3]

Approaching the Great City from the west and in view of its famous skyline, one passes through a vast expanse of wetlands and streams, industrial parks and highways, known as the Meadowlands. Strewn as it was with tires and toxic pollutants in the 1950s and 60s, it was a

---

3   Unless otherwise indicated, all text in the book, including epigraphs, incantation, and verse, is the author's own.

terrible place for a naturalist to grow up, but a good breeding ground for an environmentalist. Hog farms once gave a portion of the area a bad name and permeated the turnpike with malodors. Scum lined the water and decimated whole populations of fish. Factories, waste dumps, and chemical ponds smothered the landscape.

Today egrets, herons, ducks, and other birds are easily viewed from the train in this jumbled ecosystem, signs of a different era that has to some extent cleaned up its act. The farms have been replaced with hotels, warehouse outlets, and a major sports arena, all interspersed with bulrushes and reeds in cleaner water. The river that runs through it has improved considerably, with more fish species returning. While the crumbling elevated highway gives stark evidence that this is still part of the Rust Belt, the new construction and fresher wetlands invite, rather than jar, the eye.

Yet the Meadowlands remains a legacy of decades of degradation. The river is far from clean, with much contaminated sediment accumulated in its beds. Fish populations are nowhere near their pre-industrial levels. The landscape looks better, but it is by no means natural or harmonious. Iconic laws and regulations for clean water and clean air and toxic waste cleanup have improved the scene, but only so far. The area gives hope that human use can become more in design with nature, rather than in total disregard for it; yet the scars are so deep and pervasive that restoration seems a far-off goal.

In the broader context the intense industrialization here is being replicated worldwide in developing countries and parts of developed ones. It is happening anew on the frontier of forest, desert, and tundra, and even in the ocean. Multinational corporations are behind much of this activity, and not all are American or even European. Environmental laws and regulations that now form the protective superstructure in developed countries either do not exist or exist only on paper in developing ones. Combined with social forces such as subsistence agriculture and migration, the world's resources are under unprecedented pressure and stress. Earth's forests, freshwater bodies, estuarine and coastal habitats, wetlands, and grasslands are diminishing or being degraded each year at alarming rates.

Over the past twenty years some developed countries have begun to embrace the concept of sustainability as a positive, preemptive principle for their economies. In Europe this has been manifested in far-reaching laws prohibiting toxic substances in electronics and other products as a way of promoting greener chemistry in ordinary commerce and agriculture. The practice of producer responsibility for manufactured products and corporate social responsibility for the company as a whole have become common, if not universally accepted, aspects of business in North America and Europe.

Green products and services have infiltrated the marketplace in many categories, and green marketing claims are everywhere. Looking at the advertising, one might well wonder whether there remain any serious environmental problems warranting our concern. Corporations, at least in the developed world, seem finally to understand that society demands a shift in their values, where profits and shareholder value are not the only goals of their charter. Even the largest retailer in the world now takes sustainability seriously and has commanded companies in its supply chain to be green or be gone.

And still the world burns.

The world burns as we continue to burn up its once vast reservoir of rainforests, tropical and temperate, and clear forest and natural habitats for agriculture and development.

The world burns as we continue to burn up its once vast reservoir of fossilized fuels, raising our global temperature and rendering our climate more unstable and chaotic.

The world burns as we continue to burn the genetic material of our children and other animals as we disperse toxic chemicals throughout our planet.

And the world burns as we continue to burn through the once vast store of biodiversity and genetic heritage of all other species on the earth through mindless destruction of them and their habitats.

The Meadowlands may be a veiled harbinger of the destruction that awaits us with climate change, species and habitat loss, and pervasive toxic pollution. We have been warned for decades about the continuing deterioration, with global reports and environmental near-disasters such as the Ozone Hole. We know what needs to change, but we don't seem to know—economically, politically, or socially—*how* to stop the juggernaut of destructive development and resource depletion. In the face of a growing global population and greater material demands from its burgeoning middle class, we face the dilemma of trying to raise the world's standard of living as our material life-support system on earth nears exhaustion and possible collapse. We continue madly on this path, fully within our control, yet in reality clearly out of control. Something essential is missing or dysfunctional within us.

....

> *Our attitude toward nature is lacking in a vital way;*
> *in our destruction of nature, something is lost in our souls.*
> *We must develop sound moral and aesthetic attitudes*
> *toward nature based not on ecological knowledge so*
> *much as on human values themselves.*

This is not a call for less information and knowledge. While we have learned much in the past fifty years of the environmental movement, nature is so complex that we need even more research on ecosystems, biology, and environmental science. The uncertainty and controversy over climate change—where not merely political—reflect the extent to which our understanding of the earth's systems and dynamics is still very limited.

But more information and knowledge will not necessarily change our behavior nor cause the deniers to cease denying that we face real and critical environmental problems. What is missing is not so much in our heads, as in our hearts and souls.

To some extent, this element has been missing for a long time. Environmental problems are not new. Destruction of nature and our life-support is an old story that dogs human history. As far back as the ice ages, we decimated the mastodons and mammoths, and in the classical period we destroyed once-abundant forests surrounding the Mediterranean. Our pioneers dug up most of the rich loam soil and grasslands of the prairies for farming and felled large areas of forest in the upper Midwest for lumber and charcoal. New England by the mid-nineteenth century (prior to the opening of the Erie Canal) was largely cleared of forests for pasture and agriculture, and the South for plantations and wood. While some of these activities were certainly necessary for the survival and development of society, the extensive transformation of natural landscapes often had unintended consequences. Deforestation in the Mediterranean caused regional climate change and desertification around two thousand years ago, and the plowing of the prairies led to widespread soil erosion, sedimentation, and eventually the Dust Bowl of the 1930s.

Today we have good information on the habitat changes and destruction we are causing, on the loss in particular of tropical rainforests, on the depletion of other renewable and non-renewable resources, and on our global impacts on the stratosphere, atmosphere, climate, and ocean. We have monitoring systems and global databases for many environmental indicators, from tropical deforestation to atmospheric CO_2. While we have only a vague idea of the total number of species on the planet (anywhere from around ten million to one hundred million), we have a good idea that ecosystem destruction, particularly in the tropics, is decimating many of them at rates greater than experienced since the last major extinction sixty-five million years ago. We argue about the total supply of fossil fuels and whether we have reached peak oil, but surely all realize this reservoir is ultimately finite (despite any new discoveries) and certainly harmful as it is uncovered and burned.

The world still burns, regardless of how much we know, because we have dissociated ourselves from nature and from our humanistic values for nature.

The world still burns, regardless of how much we know, because we lack something vital in our attitude toward nature.

The world still burns, regardless of how much we know, because we have lost sight of our kinship with nature.

And the world still burns, regardless of how much we know, because our denial of nature has led to a denial of part of ourselves—perhaps the part that loves.

....

Come with me as we seek the cause for our predicament and how we can solve it. Let us journey through some recent environmental history to see how far we have come and what still keeps us from living sustainably. We'll consider the issue of responsibility and what drives us as consumers and even get philosophical in addressing root causes and solutions for our crisis. Brace for color as I dice the discussion with personal observations, vignettes, and reflections. But please stay for the conclusion.

Here is the bottom line, the headline, the sound bite: *Our relationship with nature is fundamentally a moral one. Our destruction of nature represents a violation of our most important human values as well as a threat to our survival.*

I know that morality is not a favorite subject today, that it has Victorian, religious, even chauvinistic overtones. But we must honestly recognize what is most important in our lives and bravely search for those values that are lacking. "Morality" involves deep-seated human *values* concerning our relationship and interaction with the world around us. It encompasses but far transcends "ethics," which focuses on appropriate *behavior* among human beings. This emphasis on the *humanistic values of nature* both highlights and neutralizes that which separates humans from the rest of the world. While morality may be a uniquely human value, as interpreted here it requires humans to overcome their separation from and devaluation of nature. To be a truly moral human being, to live up to our highest standards and values, we must not only appreciate nature and the world around us, but also treat them as if they were ourselves.

Because, in the final analysis, nature, the environment, the earth are indeed "us." Some dream of living on the moon or Mars, but how little regard this gives to the reality of such an environment—and to all it would lack.[4] In any case, living on another planet would still require us to consider how we treat our life support and other species that happen to come along. We cannot escape that aspect of morality and human values. Nor can we ignore any longer the so-called ecosystem services the earth provides us as part of our evolution and their increasing deterioration under our ill-managed stewardship.

Recognizing our true relationship to nature and embracing our most important values are critically important for the future of humanity and of the many other species who share the earth with us. I will not repeat the many dire warnings related to global climate change, loss of habitat and farmland, deforestation, loss of freshwater, depletion of fish stocks, and the like. Some may consider these forecasts alarmist and unfounded or believe that, even if true, humans will find ways to adapt to or overcome any resource shortages or environmental changes through our technological abilities and ingenuity. But this begs the question of whether the resulting world is one we want our descendants to be born into. Furthermore, it ignores the fact that many other animal and plant species on earth will not be able to adapt so readily and quickly and will perish—to their detriment and quite likely to ours, as well.

---

4   One is reminded here of Robert Frost's famous verse from "Birches": "Earth's the right place for love: I don't know where it's likely to go better." (Robert Frost, *Complete Poems of Robert Frost* (New York: Holt, Rinehart and Winston, 1967), 153).

Ultimately, what is critically important is that we truly attain the status of being human and what is potentially best about that. It is time for us to become the moral beings we know we should and can be. It is time for us to be truly humane in our dealings with other humans and other species. And it is time for us to stop burning the world, our life support, our fellow creatures, ourselves.

CHAPTER 2

An Historical Perspective:
From End of Pipe to All of Pipe

....

He leaned over confidentially toward me and told me in no uncertain terms: "Because you get in the way of our equity with the consumer."

I didn't know what he was talking about.

He explained further. By putting someone else's environmental seal of approval on their products, they would dilute their own brand value with consumers. They didn't want another organization to replace the trust and credibility they had built with consumers over more than a century.

A senior executive with a major consumer products company, Harold had agreed to meet with me in my office in late 1996 to explain why they not only declined to seek green certification for their products, but opposed the very basis for such approval. They had, in fact, initiated a high-level campaign to discredit all third-party ecolabeling programs around the world. It appeared that the nascent movement to green the economy faced possible extinction from an icon of American capitalism before it even got off the ground.

For decades before, from the late 1960s to the early 1990s, the environmental movement in the United States had prosecuted companies for the pollution they emitted to air, water, and land. Environmental laws and regulations and the many advocacy groups formed to monitor and promote their enforcement were adversarial in nature and usually punitive after-the-fact. Companies were considered bad actors whose behavior had to be controlled through stringent limits on their discharges (such as in water or air permits) and the threat of serious fines or even criminal charges for excessive pollution. Throughout, the focus of attention was on what came out at the end of the industrial process—at the end of the pipe.[5]

This was not a misplaced emphasis, given what had happened over the course of twentieth-century industrialization: dozens of deaths from factory air pollution in Donora, Pennsylvania (1948); the Great Smog of London that killed thousands from coal burning (1952); Cuyahoga River in Ohio that burst into flames from floating chemicals and debris (1969); the toxic

---

5   Regulations under the Clean Water Act made determinations of allowable limits on discharged pollutants for each major industry sector, and these were applied to specific factories through the National Pollutant Discharge Elimination System (NPDES) permits. Under both the Clean Water Act and the Clean Air Act the best technologies for industrial production and cleanup processes were examined and used as the basis for these determinations, but the focus was on how these technologies affected what came out at the end of the wastewater pipe or smokestack. In terms of solid and hazardous waste, RCRA (the disposal law) and Superfund (the cleanup law) considered how end-of-process residuals were disposed of by companies and municipalities or remediated afterward. Only the toxic substances law (TSCA) looked at chemicals used upfront in production, but its actual reach and effectiveness were severely limited.

industrial waste horror of Love Canal that seeped into families' homes (late 1970s); the infamous smog of Los Angeles from millions of vehicles (ongoing); countless fish kills from streams polluted by mines or untreated sewage; and so on. Almost all these incidents came from pollution, and most came from a pipe, or at least from the end of an industrial or technological process. It made perfect sense to control these emissions in terms of the dangerous pollutants or toxic substances they contained.

Integrating Prevention Upfront

In the late 1980s and early 1990s a new approach emerged. Keep the limitations and punishments, but encourage and reward industry's good behavior. Better yet, work with companies to help them do the right thing. That led logically to looking at the entire production process and seeing where improvements could be made from the start to avoid problems at the end. Soon the concept of life-cycle assessment came to the fore—analyzing a product or material for its environmental impacts from raw material extraction through production to use and end-of-life management. Other concepts such as cleaner production, design for the environment, and green chemistry took shape, all part of a fundamental change in how the economy was supposed to function and how its products and services would be judged.

This dichotomy between damage control after the fact versus a more integrated, preventative approach is not confined to environmental protection, as was brought home to me personally and poignantly when our toddler son became stricken with a life-threatening disease. After a month of daily treatments he was declared temporarily free of disease; we asked what we should be doing next to keep him that way, and the doctors (who thankfully cured the immediate problem) had no answer. It took my wife Rebecca several years of tirelessly researching, learning, and experimenting to discover all the preventative measures that could be taken to restore and maintain his health through holistic nutrition and alternative medicine. By considering a person's health in an integrated way, these approaches can provide numerous proactive measures for maintaining health and preventing chronic disease.

The Sustainable Economy and the Rise of Ecolabeling
In 1987 the United Nations Brundtland commission issued its celebrated report on development and the environment. It espoused the concept of sustainable development, which it defined as developing and managing the economy in a way that meets our needs but does not compromise the needs of future generations. Sustainability became the catch-all concept for a more holistic approach that integrated environmental and health concerns upfront and upstream in the economy. A revolution was underway.

Around this time a few advocacy groups that had spent the previous two decades suing companies for their pollution began working with them to improve their product design and production processes. One group worked with a large fast-food chain to help it reduce its solid waste and streamline its food packaging. Another worked less visibly with a major chemical and intermediary manufacturer in so-called pollution prevention projects that redesigned production processes and raw materials to achieve significant savings and waste reductions. Other groups and companies took notice.

Also in the late 1980s (though a decade earlier in Germany) a movement arose in Europe and North America to identify so-called green products through seals or ecolabels. Since the economy is ultimately comprised of its products and services, a sustainable economy must have sustainable products or services. These ecolabeling programs developed environmental standards for specific categories of products and services based on their life-cycle impacts and the best-in-class in the market. Products and services that met the standards would be certified and allowed to use the ecolabels. Environmentally conscious consumers would know which products to buy, and manufacturers with certified products would gain market share and increased sales. It seemed a sure winner to reward companies with these ecolabels for incorporating a more sustainable approach to the way they did business.

By the early 1990s North America offered two general ecolabels (Green Seal in the United States, Environmental Choice in Canada), and Europe had several, including one for the entire European Union (EU Flower). More specific environmental labels focusing on particular attributes (e.g., Energy Star) or resources (e.g., Forest Stewardship Council) also sprang up in this period.[6] Although uptake in the US market was initially slow, the response in Canada and Europe suggested that ecolabeling and the green economy revolution it symbolized were taking hold, and fast. Even the august and conservative International Organization for Standardization (ISO), in recognition of this growing momentum, initiated a project in 1993 to develop guidelines for environmental practices in the marketplace—including environmental labeling.

....

---

6   Although these latter environmental labels are not holistic or fully life-cycle-based, they all share the concept of looking upstream in the economy and promoting more sustainable practices, designs, and materials.

> *Mr. Chairman.*
> *Not Japanese*
> *I'm a Korean.*
> —*Delegate's note to ISO 14020 Working Group Convener*

Pierre met me at a café on the Left Bank. We had agreed to get together before the ISO meeting in Paris in 1994 to map our strategy to prevent Green Seal and similar programs from getting reamed by industry in the ISO standards addressing third-party ecolabeling programs.

ISO was formed just after World War II to harmonize commercial standards around the world. Most of its efforts are quite esoteric and not in the least earth-shaking, such as standardizing the sizes of screws or the methods for measuring ingredients. Other than a foray in the 1980s into quality management systems, its scope was hard-core, nuts and bolts, industrial, not fringe or controversial. This new project in the environmental arena, which focused on environmental management systems but included environmental labeling, life-cycle assessment, and related areas, put ISO way out of its element, and its normal procedures proved largely inadequate to cope with the controversies and broad array of interests involved.

Like most ISO groups, the working group for environmental labels was comprised predominantly of multinational corporations, along with a number of government representatives, but included just a few non-profit environmental and consumer organizations. Pierre was the European representative of a large international environmental group, which had a particular interest in independent forest certification in addition to more general ecolabels like Green Seal. Other than someone from the global association of ecolabeling programs, he and I represented the non-industry, non-governmental world in this effort to standardize green product labeling internationally.

As a federation of national standards bodies, ISO counted on each country's delegation to provide the staff for working groups and their conveners. The US delegation was, of course, the largest and most influential. Almost all its members were major corporations, their consultants, government agencies, and standard developers, working under the coordination of the American national standards body.

When Green Seal joined this ISO project in 1993, we were not only an outlier; we were an outcast. The attitude of most of the rest of the US delegation was palpably cool to this environmental group with "green" in its name. The other standards bodies, who worked with industry to set good practice (baseline) standards, looked down on us and kept their distance. Only one or two people from a few companies reached out to us.

The US delegation managed to get a plum: Of the three sub-working groups on environmental labels, the US could pick the convener of the one developing general principles of environmental labels (dubbed ISO 14020), thus setting the tone for the others focusing on specific types of environmental labeling.[7] They were about to name an industry person to this important position, as they had for several working groups in other areas, when one of the company people who had reached out to me strongly pleaded with his colleagues to choose me. Frank, the representative of a large paper company, argued that these ISO standards would lack credibility with the environmental community and the public at large if they were completely

---

7   Initially, these included Type 1, for ecolabels from third-party programs based on multiple leadership criteria and covering many product categories; Type 2, for self-declarations by manufacturers; and Type 3, a kind of report card on multiple attributes without criteria.

dominated by industry. Reluctantly, the US delegation accepted his argument and appointed me as convener.

This was actually a mixed blessing. As international convener, I was supposed to remain neutral and facilitate the development of the work product. While Green Seal was accustomed to dealing with many stakeholders and viewpoints in developing our own standards, we always had the final say. This would not be the case here. But as convener I could exert some control on the issues discussed and determine when agreement was reached by working group members.

Pierre and I hit it off on a personal level, making it easier to bridge the occasional differences in our viewpoints and organizational positions. He was a young Swiss national, and I had lived and taught in Switzerland two decades before in Suisse Romande, his native region (though I rarely dared to speak French with him, so rusty had it become). At the café we quickly agreed on the situation we faced. We were vastly outnumbered even in the international working groups (which mirrored the national ones). Industry, which had not yet accepted the green revolution, would push to water down ecolabeling standards and make them easy to meet or not very meaningful. They would use tactics and arguments that seemed reasonable but could thwart true leadership in defining what is green. At the worst, they would create an impressive international structure for greenwashing the *status quo*—making things look more environmentally responsible than they really are.

About the only area where Pierre and I did not see eye-to-eye was the position of developing countries. Already, through some criteria in European ecolabeling programs, manufacturers in developing countries claimed they were denied access to ecolabels and put at an economic disadvantage. In the most egregious cases these producers had to source materials for their products in ways that were clearly not environmentally beneficial, such as by importing recycled fiber from Europe to meet European ecolabeling paper standards. Pierre's group staunchly supported developing countries and fought so-called environmental injustice. But those of us in the ecolabeling programs saw the multinational corporations and some national standards developers seizing on this issue as a way of attacking us. It put us in an awkward position, indeed, to be seen as opposing developing countries.

Worse, industry was developing a huge wedge to compromise the leadership aspects of ecolabeling—requiring that ecolabeling standards be developed through consensus, meaning that stakeholders involved generally agree on all the requirements in the standards. This would potentially undermine the very mechanism by which ecolabeling makes markets greener.

The whole idea of ecolabeling is to identify and promote those products (and services) that meet high levels of environmental and health performance in their particular market sectors. By definition, this should be a minority of the products in each sector and represent leadership. By being awarded an ecolabel, such products can theoretically gain market share, with the idea that manufacturers will strive to make other products meet the leadership levels of ecolabeling standards, leading to market transformation. All this is premised on having standards with leadership levels.

In fact, developing leadership standards for most product categories is very difficult precisely because of the tension between setting high levels, which most products and manufacturers do not meet (by definition), and considering the viewpoints of all stakeholders (including manufacturers) in an open and transparent process. While this kind of process puts great value on listening to and incorporating to the extent possible everyone's positions and concerns, the goal of ecolabeling standards is always to set leadership levels. Leadership cannot be compromised even for the sake of achieving consensus among the stakeholders involved.

For commercial standards developed by national and international standards bodies like ISO, consensus is king. The goal of every working group is to achieve consensus for the standard, or else it is not promulgated. This ensures broad acceptance of the standard, but it also means that the standard will reflect a number of compromises that potentially diminish its effect. For controversial and sometimes uncertain areas such as environmental and health protection, adherence to a consensus process virtually ensures that a standard will be watered down to a level of minimal or acceptable performance, not leadership.

Industry argued in the ISO process that ecolabeling standards should be based on consensus. They figured that no one could successfully oppose consensus, not only because it was institutionally ingrained in ISO but also because it is such a sympathetic concept. Developing countries, seeing consensus as leverage in their fight with European ecolabels, seized on the idea. Unwary non-profit groups at the fringe of the process (and increasingly being wooed by the US delegation) nodded their assent. Pierre understood immediately what was afoot and fought hard with me to counter this pernicious attack.

In the end several years later, after serious opposition by Pierre's group and the ecolabeling association, my ISO working group reached the following consensus on the issue of developing ecolabeling standards: "Reasonable efforts should be made to achieve a consensus. . . ." This meant that we would have to *try* to achieve consensus for our standards, as we already customarily practiced, but we would *not be forced* to compromise their leadership levels for consensus. Achieving consensus, in other words, was not the end in itself. Score one for the green economy.

....

As she lay dying. . .

I dropped my urgent personal letter in the Grand Central post office and hurried east. I had grossly misjudged the walking distance from Penn Station, thinking in conventional, not New York, terms, and was in danger of being late for my lunch meeting with the foundations. The three hundred block of 43rd Street was not just three blocks from Fifth Avenue, but more like five, with each block more than twice the normal length.

Harold's company had not been idle in dealing with the threat they saw in ecolabeling. About a year before I met with him in my office, they formed a coalition of industry trade associations to discredit and destroy ecolabeling programs world-wide. The coalition issued a manifesto that said, in a favorite right-wing phrase of the day, that ecolabeling is "fundamentally flawed." It argued that environmental science is not sufficiently advanced to allow for definitive standards for green products; moreover, that environmental impacts are regionally distributed and a matter of personal values—someone in the US Southwest might be more concerned with water than solid waste, while the reverse would be true in the Northeast—so it would be impossible to set a valid national standard.[8]

---

8   These arguments have a grain of truth but are not irrefutable and certainly do not invalidate ecolabeling. Environmental science, product science, and life-cycle assessment have been able to address significant environmental and health impacts of products and potential trade-offs among them. Industry scientists unconstrained by corporate politics can usually agree on these with other stakeholders. As to geographic variations, all national standards

The group Harold's company formed was sanctimoniously named the Coalition for Truth in Environmental Marketing Information. A decade or two before, similar interests aligned against controls on natural resource use formed the equally euphemistic Wise Use Movement. The Coalition for Truth boasted a membership of about thirteen major associations representing a range of industry sectors from grocery manufacturers (spearheaded by Harold's company) to electronics to paper companies. They hired a former general counsel of the US Environmental Protection Agency to lobby the US government not to procure products simply because of their ecolabels. Meeting one-on-one in Washington with mid-level bureaucrats responsible for green purchasing policy in EPA, the lobbyist threatened them with the argument that specifying a third-party seal for government purchasing was an abrogation of a constitutionally "inherent government function." (He did not explain how the federal government was allowed to contract out management of its nuclear production facilities to a third party.)

The lunch meeting in late March 1996 was arranged hastily to alert the foundation community, which had supported our program and others like it, about the growing menace of the Coalition for Truth, and to make a plan for countering it. There was a good probability they would fund the counter-coalition we were proposing, and we also had the backing of a few large environmental groups. I got to the door just before noon, out of

essentially average these out, and in any case the purpose of leadership sustainability standards is to minimize adverse impacts across the life cycle (e.g., it is still beneficial to minimize water use in the Northeast and solid waste in the Southwest) and to optimize among necessary tradeoffs. As to personal values, a major benefit of national policies and standards is that they transcend personal preferences and address priorities from a national or societal perspective.

breath and moist with sweat under my suit. I soon discovered that the foundation's dining room was perched at the top of the building over the huge atrium, with nothing below it for ten floors. This added to the anxiety I already felt over this critical meeting. I had to focus on Fran and Michael at the table before me, not the emptiness below me or the East River out the window. I explained in measured but forceful terms what was evolving in the marketplace and the threat the Coalition for Truth posed to the green economy movement. I tried not to let my mind wander to other things. . .

Dear Brenda and Cuthbert: I am writing to notify you that Peggy is dying of cancer. She really wants to hear from you—as soon as possible, if you could. I know that reaching her from Zimbabwe may be difficult, but there is little time left. . .

Fran and Michael asked many tough questions, but they seemed engaged and concerned. We talked about the plan, and at the end of lunch they invited a proposal for funding the counter-coalition. I felt relieved, exhilarated, and glad to walk the cantilevered platform over to the elevator down.

Immediately on returning to Washington we put our initial counter-coalition and the foundation proposal together. We worked feverishly, feeling there was little time to waste, given the Coalition for Truth's inroads with the federal government and its increasing reach internationally. I drafted a first cut at the proposal, which went the rounds of management review in our organization. We had meetings with our partners, including two major environmental groups. Although they had more interest in protecting forest certification than product certification, everyone saw eye-to-eye about the critical need for this counter-coalition and the role it would play. Almost everything was coming together, at least at work. . .

When I left the hospice, knowing it would be for the last time, I walked past my car and instinctively climbed up the embankment behind the lot. There, opened panoramically before me, lay the Branford marshes, so dear to her heart and beside which she would be buried in a matter of days. . . .

The Consumers' Choice Council, as our counter-coalition came to be called, employed a number of psychological tricks of its own. We had a good name, politically correct but accurate. Chad, whom we hired to direct the campaign, fought the enemy with food—thoughtful dinners for influential people in sustainable restaurants, and well-catered conferences on constructive topics in the field. He countered not with verbal sallies or polemics, nor with issue papers or debates. He created art around ecolabeling and fellowship around green products. At first I was somewhat troubled, but I saw soon how winning were his ways.

The Consumers' Choice Council on balance neutralized the Coalition for Truth in Environmental Marketing Information. The latter did inflict damage—some of it serious and long-lasting. In particular, the intense, threatening lobbying created a negative image toward ecolabeling and our organization in the minds of federal staff for a number of years. They became cool if not antagonistic toward us and sought every means to avoid specifying our standards, to the detriment of federal procurement.

On the international front we came to more of a draw, even a win. Considering how they might have come out, the ISO guidelines represented a victory. In the World Trade Organization, which looked at ecolabeling with a jaundiced eye because of possible barriers to trade, we avoided potentially devastating edicts. The council worked with the

US trade representative and other countries to present our viewpoint and the value of ecolabeling for the green economy. A working group of the WTO was convened to study the issue of ecolabeling and its effects on trade, but its report merely flagged the possibility of harm and did not recommend controls or sanctions.

Eventually, in the late 1990s, we heard less and less of the Coalition for Truth. Their lobbyist moved on. They did not speak at conferences, and their destructive articles no longer appeared. Our council would fold up, too, having achieved its purpose. As the millennium turned, the way seemed clear for the green economy to emerge. Notwithstanding a recession and major terrorist attack on the United States, companies began to talk in the early 2000s as if sustainability were, indeed, an integral part of their business. Green standards started taking hold in the world's largest economy.

Market Transformation Begins

I gave a talk in early 2002 at a conference in Philadelphia, held in a hotel we had just certified on Rittenhouse Square. We had partnered the year before with the Commonwealth of Pennsylvania to certify hotels around the state, so this offered an opportunity to showcase the program. Moreover, at lunch I would meet with a group of state purchasers and other experts who wanted to interview me to see whether our program, particularly our cleaning products standard, was worthy of citing in Massachusetts's upcoming bid for such products.

Mike, our marketing head, had worked with our research partner at the University of Tennessee in the late 1990s to complete the cleaning products standard for the US Army's base in Aberdeen, Maryland, to use on its thousands of buildings.

I was tied up in serious organizational issues at the time, and our staff had dwindled in number. Although Mike gallantly took on overseeing the standards project, I was a little worried about how it was developing, given its potential significance. Fortunately, despite the reticence of a few industry associations to participate, the standard came out splendidly—not only as leadership, but also as consensus.

Marcia and Eric of Massachusetts's procurement division drilled me about our organization, our standards development process, and the cleaning products standard itself. I could barely get a bite in between remarks. I wasn't sure how well I was received, although I could answer most questions satisfactorily. The toughest was why we hadn't yet certified any products to this standard. It takes time to enter the marketplace, I replied; we're part of a major cultural change; we have some products under review. Was that skepticism in their eyes?

Months later Massachusetts issued its "RFR"—a "Request for Response for Cleaning Products, Environmentally Preferable (Reduced Health and Environmental Impacts)." It cited Green Seal's standard and required for many sub-categories that products for bid meet its criteria! The news flashed around the industry and the budding green purchasing community. An ecolabeling standard was actually being used for the specifications of a major institution's purchasing.

While not a large state, Massachusetts was very influential in the procurement world, and it had regional significance in the marketplace. Soon we started receiving more applications for certification. Companies did not have to get their cleaning products certified to make a bid to the state, but they would have to prove they met our standard's criteria. Over the next few years the certifications increased exponentially, as other states and government agencies followed Massachusetts's lead in specifying our standards for cleaning products, paint, and other categories.

The broader marketplace experienced a similar surge in green certifications in the early to mid-2000s decade. This was especially true for green building certification, but also for energy and electronics labels. A number of our sister ecolabeling programs around the world saw a similar uptake of their programs in the marketplace. Around 2005-6 the green economy gained further momentum as climate change captured popular attention with Hurricane Katrina's devastation of New Orleans and Gore's documentary *An Inconvenient Truth*. Companies started to take sustainability seriously at the corporate as well as product level, and corporate social responsibility became the new buzzwords for a holistic approach to company behavior that put environmental and social considerations almost at par with economic ones.

The decades-old arguments of industry against environmental policies and the green economy began to drop off. Less frequently did we get identical comments on our standards, clearly drafted by a trade association, from different company stakeholders. Concepts such as risk assessment did not disappear, but industry was less wont to use them as weapons against progress. We felt more comfortable promoting the precautionary principle, which supports prohibitions on chemicals or technologies which are potentially harmful even if evidence is insufficient either way.

Industry scientists still raised the distinction between the hazard a material may cause and its actual risk of harm based on likely exposure, the combination of which forms classical risk assessment. And, in fairness, there were situations where we took likely exposures into account. But to build a green economy it was necessary to weed out the bad chemicals and start anew with safer ingredients—not to see how far one could still employ the harmful ones under likely exposure scenarios. After all, humans are not good at predicting unknown risks and consequences. Who would have thought that underarm spray or refrigerators would eat stratospheric ozone?

By the time of the financial crash of 2008 green product claims were rampant in the marketplace, and so was greenwashing with questionable environmental claims. Companies vied to demonstrate their social responsibility and greenness, and while this was not always accompanied by their producing green products, much less by having them certified, the number of ecolabeled products and services was increasing rapidly. The elements were in place for a true transition—really, a transformation—to the green economy. Finally, business and consumers seemed truly to understand. And yet . . .

Tropical forests still fell and burned.
Carbon gases expanded from the flues.
Toxic chemicals seared our children's brains.
Species withered in lost habitats.

Somewhere, among all these companies supposedly practicing corporate social responsibility and green production, the exploitation continued apace. Who, or what, was responsible? And how could it be stopped?

CHAPTER 3

Responsible Parties: Who Makes the Economy Green?

....

Few of us realize that with every plug, tissue, shower, flush, meal, mop, load, or trip we cause an impact on the earth and potentially on our health. The environmentally conscious among us have internalized this concept and exhibit it in their spartan lifestyles. They turn off the lights behind you and set the thermostat down when you aren't looking. They may or may not nag their living mates, but they are sure to cringe at the waste they see around them. In actuality, most of us don't want to think about these things, much less live austerely. Americans, especially, do not take kindly to sacrificing their affluence without a compelling reason.

In large part we have gained this blissful ignorance honestly. For decades the modern environmental movement has focused either on industry's polluting ways or on conservation of distant wildlands. The emphasis has long been on end-of-pipe problems and solutions, including toxic waste and pesticides in the environment, along with exploitation or protection of wilderness and primeval forest, or the occasional marquee species that is endangered. These are all real and important problems, and they are the basis for lament. But the connection to our everyday lives is rarely illuminated, typically only when an environmental catastrophe strikes home.

This has led to the demonization of industry, and not entirely fairly. Certainly industry has been responsible for widespread pollution, wanton resource use, and serious societal harm. Environmental advocacy groups realized early on that corporate polluters made highly effective campaign targets and, not irrelevantly, good fund-raisers. But by making industry synonymous with pollution, people could believe that stronger laws and enforcement to bring "the polluters" in line would solve all problems. The smokestacks, the dumps, the clearcuts could be eliminated, and our environment would be restored. The extent to which industry serves and reflects society's needs and material wants was conveniently ignored. People could think that the root cause of environmental problems was out there— someone else's responsibility.

Our Everyday Connection through Consumption

Let us look briefly at the connections between our lives and the environment, to dispel any remaining ignorance or skepticism. On the macro level it is estimated that Americans, while only five percent of humanity, consume around a quarter of the world's resources. If the current world population of seven billion were to live at the same material level, we would need the equivalent of five earths to produce the food, housing, and materials for this lifestyle. Our economic engine is driven by fossil fuels that have enormous impacts in their extraction, processing, and consumption; by metals and minerals that must be mined, processed, and transported; and by a complex network of material flows and transportation.

On the micro scale, in our everyday life, the connections are numerous and complex. Turn on the switch and you are using energy that comes most likely from a fossil fuel—coal, oil, or natural gas; even hydropower affects habitat and fish populations, while nuclear power is a controversial subject unto itself. Turn on the automobile and you are using fossil fuel, emitting air pollutants and significant amounts of greenhouse gases, and embracing a major supply chain of materials, parts, and production. Turn on the clothes washer and you are using lots of energy (unless you use a cold-water wash), detergents that may have toxins harmful to humans and aquatic species, and of course packaging material that may wind up in a landfill. Turn on the stove and you are cooking something that likely took abundant amounts of fossil fuels and petrochemicals to produce and transport.

For your more intimate moments the tissue you use has been derived from trees, sometimes virgin forest or plantations that replaced them, and produced in a highly energy-, water-, and chemical-intensive process to give the desired softness and whiteness. Your baths, showers, and flushes all consume precious freshwater (itself purified with chemicals like chlorine) and (in the first two instances) fossil fuels, and they all become wastewater that has to be treated with more chemicals before discharge to streams. Your soaps, lotions, and cosmetics come from chemicals, often petroleum-derived, that may actually be harmful to you as well as to aquatic species, which receive the residues that eventually go down the drain. And your clothing derives either from petrochemical synthetics or from natural fibers that are intensively cultivated (with pesticides and fertilizers) and processed (with chemicals and dyes) before they are assembled in overseas sweatshops under frequently unsanitary and unsafe conditions.

This catalogue may serve as a wakeup call for many, a reminder for others. But one should not feel guilty. The guilt trip was tried early on, and it did not work. People don't like feeling guilty, especially about things that have been positively reinforced in their lives through ubiquitous marketing and advertising. People also won't feel guilty if they cannot readily see a viable alternative to the conventional actions they are criticized for taking.

Can Consumers Change Our Production System?

We are all part of a system that was developed to promote production and consumption to achieve economic growth and the prosperity that supposedly comes with it. Knowing that you are part of this system can provide more leverage and make you a force for positive change. Sensitivity to your purchases and activities can certainly help reduce your impacts. And, of course, understanding better the nature of these impacts and discerning which products and activities have lesser or worse impacts can enable you to reduce your footprint.

That has essentially been the strategy of the green economy movement in the past twenty years. Show consumers which products are preferable for their health and the environment, and they will buy them over more harmful conventional ones. After all, survey after survey from the 1990s on has shown that a high percentage of consumers (up to eighty percent) is willing to buy green products. Or, at least, they say they are.

Actually, only a small percentage, less than ten percent, does. The reasons for this large discrepancy are numerous: green products often cost more; green products are often considered less effective (despite near parity in recent years); green products are often hard to find in stores; and green products are difficult to identify in many categories. Most of all, as we have just seen, consumers typically *do not think* about environmental matters or even health issues when buying products or services. And why should they, if they are not used to making the connections and don't feel responsible for them?

A Culture Change in Procurement

Even professional purchasers—those who buy goods and services for use by government agencies, companies, or institutions like hospitals or universities—are only beginning to incorporate environmental and health criteria in their specifications as a routine matter. In our frequent dealings with such purchasers over the past fifteen years we have seen a marked increase in their attention to the sustainability aspects of procurement, but it is by no means yet established as an integral part of their work. Even the US government, which mandated the incorporation of environmental considerations in purchasing in an executive order back in 1993, has taken many years to implement this policy, and it is still quite limited in the scope of product categories it covers.

The professional procurement world, in fact, represents a microcosm of the culture change we see more broadly in society. Professional purchasers are trained to consider performance, quality, and cost in specifying products, as well as to ensure that the process is transparent and legitimate. Environmental or sustainability criteria for products are essentially alien concepts. One of the biggest challenges purchasers have faced, in trying to incorporate environmental criteria on top of the other big three, is that lowest cost is traditionally the deciding criterion once performance and quality criteria are met. Many procurement regulations and policies have had to be modified to allow cost premiums to consider certain green products or even to change the decision criteria to "best value" from lowest cost. Under a best-value approach higher product cost may be offset by better environmental performance, or a higher initial cost of a product may be offset by lower maintenance costs or so-called life-cycle (cumulative) costs.[9] In any case, a very different way of thinking and of evaluating products is required from the traditional procurement approach.

Several projects Green Seal undertook in California in the past decade illustrate well the challenges and opportunities in re-orienting large institutional purchasers to green procurement. For the procurement division of the state of California, then the seventh largest economy in the world, we attempted to institutionalize green procurement in a year-long project starting in 2002. The very first task was to set priorities among the hundreds of product and service categories the state purchases so the greening effort would have the most immediate benefits. Using an innovative approach considering environmental impact, impact improvement potential, and magnitude of spending, our team came up with a list of the top fifty categories,

---

9   In many cases, traditional procurement policy has not even allowed life-cycle cost to be considered, so that a product whose higher maintenance costs far outweigh its lower initial cost would still have to be purchased over an otherwise equivalent product at higher initial cost but much lower maintenance or life-cycle cost.

headed by . . . lowly bathroom tissue and paper towels![10] We then developed various guidances for the state on how to incorporate environmental criteria into purchasing; provided criteria and lists of products meeting them for several of the priority categories; and reached out to many agencies, departments, and boards to identify their various roles in procurement and help coordinate green procurement throughout the state. The project was a good start, and some of this information became part of the procurement process, but lack of follow up and a political change in administration limited the culture change we sought to create.

The other California projects were similarly ambitious. The county of Los Angeles, the largest in the United States, passed a directive in 2007 to implement green purchasing by adopting environmental standards for products and instituting procedures to ensure that environmentally preferable products are procured. The county asked Green Seal to help it develop a five-year plan for achieving these goals. We started again with a modified prioritization scheme, then laid out the plan in terms of forty priority product categories and identified or developed leadership criteria for each of the categories. We also had to ensure that the county's policies and procedures supported environmentally preferable specifications.

Moving down the government hierarchy, a few years later Green Seal helped the city of Los Angeles develop a similar Green Purchasing Action Plan to implement a city ordinance requiring the purchase of environmentally preferable products.

---

10   This is not as surprising as it may sound. These products are used ubiquitously and plentifully, and they derive from a material that, while renewable, is critical to ecosystems and habitat; moreover, paper production is highly energy- and water-intensive and uses strong chemicals for bleaching and other processes.

In addition to setting priorities among the many categories of products purchased, the plan addressed necessary changes in the city's procurement policies and procedures to implement green purchasing, including changes in contract language, education and coordination of all agencies, and monitoring adoption of the new approach.

Reaching Consumers through Health

As tentative and novice as most of them are in incorporating sustainability criteria, professional purchasers are way ahead of the vast majority of consumers. The culture change we seek in the seventy percent of the economy dependent on consumers arises but slowly. It glimmers in the Energy Star products proliferating in electronics stores, the organic products emerging on grocery shelves, and the concentrated detergents everyone must buy. Consumers seem most likely to jump on the green bandwagon if it protects their health and that of their families. This may seem like mere self-interest, but it is a real and legitimate connection to the mix of impacts we call environmental. Fortunately, products that are more protective of human health tend to be more environmentally protective as well, although the correlation is not exact. So both kinds of benefits can be achieved through the same concern.

Advocacy groups have used the hook of human health to some effect, especially with personal-care products, but it has not been sufficient to foment the green economy revolution. Consumers—the majority of whom are women, many of them mothers—certainly care about health. The challenge, again, is to make the connection upfront between purchasing a product and its effect on health. Health issues can get very technical, so it is not at all clear what products or ingredients should be sought or avoided. The common dictum to avoid products whose ingredients you cannot pronounce provides clear but unhelpful guidance, as many acceptable ingredients fall into this category (recall aspirin's chemical name). Moreover, lay people do not necessarily want to get into the technical details, even if they could understand them. In fact, neither do most professional purchasers, which is why a third-party label and standard can be so useful. Ultimately, those who design and formulate products must ensure they are as sustainable as possible. Manufacturers, that is.

Producers Must Take the Lead

As the frontline of the economy, producers bear a special responsibility to get it right from the start. After all, if no products in a given market sector are made sustainably, consumers have no way to lessen their individual impact other than by opting out, if that is even feasible. Manufacturers in theory have the technical know-how and resources to design with the environment and health in mind.

Granted, as with purchasers, consideration of environmental impacts and chronic human health effects is new to manufacturers and requires a culture change of their own. We have seen many instances where manufacturers struggle to get the data necessary to meet these new requirements, and often they must turn to their suppliers or their suppliers' suppliers to obtain the information.[11] They may not even know that a raw

---

11   Curiously, many raw material suppliers limit what their customers, the product manufacturers, can know about their materials for reasons of business confidentiality. Raw material suppliers must comply with the minimal disclosure requirements of material safety data sheets (MSDSs) per OSHA regulations, but finding out more about their materials often requires a third-party certifier to go directly to them, not to the product manufacturers, and usually under a separate confidentiality agreement.

material contains a probable carcinogen or mutagen or that it is toxic to aquatic life. The culture of manufacturing, product design, and product management has not traditionally included these considerations. At most, when it comes to human health, manufacturers have had to ensure their products are not acutely toxic, hazardous, or dangerous. Nevertheless, the leap to more comprehensive human health attributes and environmental effects should be within the capability (whether in-house or contracted out) of all but the smallest companies. Moreover, we would expect manufacturers to seek this information when they bring a product to market in our more environmentally challenged world.

That is the rationale for a recent movement known as Extended Producer Responsibility. EPR is a policy that makes the manufacturer of a product responsible for the impacts of a product throughout its life cycle, not just up to the factory gate. EPR has been applied primarily to the end-life stages of a product, namely, waste management or product take-back; it requires manufacturers to set up programs to capture products after they are used by consumers. More popular in Europe, EPR has in fact been fought by US industry, which tried to rename and redefine it as Extended *Product* Responsibility to reflect the shared responsibility of consumers for proper use and disposal or recycling of products. Certainly there is a grain of truth in this reconfiguring, but shades of the Coalition for Truth as well.

In reality, both manufacturers and consumers are responsible for making the economy more sustainable—as well as raw material suppliers, transporters, purchasers, retailers, policymakers, and everyone else who participates in the economy or any aspect of the product and service life cycle. Each group has a role in selection or design that contributes to the economy's overall environmental and health footprint. We assert the primary role of manufacturers in this regard. But consumers and institutional purchasers can exert significant pressure on manufacturers through their choices, and the aggregation of individual demand or institutional bids for more sustainable products does affect what producers provide to the marketplace.

We often hear companies complain in a number of industries or product categories that they don't produce a green offering because consumers don't demand it. We may bemoan the passivity and lack of leadership this attitude reflects, but it is a legitimate aspect of the conventional market where supply responds to demand.[12] In the converse, where consumers show a growing interest in products or services that are sustainable, smart producers act quickly to fill the order and phase out more conventional lines, as in the emergence of lower-volatility (VOC) paints.

Retailers as Green Gatekeepers

Retailers play an increasingly powerful role in the green economy. They are the gatekeeper for consumers by pre-selecting which products appear on shelves for consumers to buy. The retail people responsible for these decisions are even called buyers, and they are among the most powerful staff of the retailer. Existing and prospective suppliers to retailers meet with these buyers in make-or-break sessions often in small rooms that resemble interrogation chambers. For large manufacturers a particular retailer may be their largest customer. For small producers a

---

12   This is certainly not always the case. John Kenneth Galbraith argued that our form of corporate capitalism and consumer culture actually depends on manufacturers creating demand for material goods on the part of consumers. Apple provides a special and telling example of this in the digital age.

retailer's decision may result in access to a large market or, if their wares are rejected, unlikely prospects for their business.

Fortunately, a number of major retailers now take seriously their role as gatekeepers of sustainability. This wasn't always the case. Ten years ago only one or two acknowledged the connection between sustainability and what they put on their shelves and then only with respect to a few products or commodities like wood. The largest among them even refused to participate in a small survey Green Seal conducted in 2003 on the extent to which retailers incorporated sustainability considerations in their buying. But several years later that same retailer turned around completely, announcing that it now considered sustainability to be a critical aspect of its business. Today it leads the charge by imposing a number of sustainability criteria on its suppliers, and it is the driving force behind a consortium of retailers, manufacturers, and universities that is developing sustainability criteria for the thousands of product categories it buys and sells.

Policymakers Play a Role

Policymakers can also help drive the green economy. As mentioned earlier in this chapter, the Federal Executive Order of 1993 (12873) spurred the revolution by mandating that federal procurement give preference to products that have a reduced effect on human health and the environment. Despite delays and lethargy in implementing this and subsequent federal green procurement policies, the federal government has had an effect on the marketplace because of its huge purchasing power (around a half trillion dollars each year). Similar policies at the state and local levels, whose collective purchasing power is at least as large, have also been influential, as we saw in the last chapter in the case of Massachusetts. In some cases green procurement has actually been mandated by law for certain categories or situations, as in the now-classic 2005 New York State law (S5435) requiring use of green cleaning products in all public and private primary and secondary schools in the state.

Nonetheless, identifying, producing, and purchasing green products remain an enormously complex task in our economy. The very novelty of it all, combined with the culture change it requires, makes it difficult for any party or parties to manage it. Even if consumers and institutional purchasers fully considered sustainability in their choices, the issues are too complex and the information too inaccessible to put entirely in their hands. Manufacturers may be the frontline of responsible choice, but they are deeply influenced by the actions and preferences of other parties in the marketplace (consumers, raw material suppliers, retailers, policymakers). Somehow sustainability must be built into the economy so that it becomes common practice— the default in most manufacturing and buying situations.

Building Sustainability into the Economy

We have touched on the various strategies and instruments for building a more sustainable economy, including laws and regulations, institutional policies and mandates, and voluntary programs like ecolabels and certification. Certainly, mandatory approaches can be the most effective, provided they actually take a comprehensive and rigorous approach to sustainability. For example, the first federal executive order on green procurement disappointed many because it (and subsequent agency guidance) provided little actual direction or criteria to enable federal purchasers to identify environmentally preferable products. Moreover, where it did get specific, in regard to copy paper, the order mandated criteria only for recycled content and left untouched the more controversial issue of chlorine bleaching. In contrast, the New York State law requiring use of green cleaning products in schools referenced third-party ecolabeling standards that are comprehensive and cutting edge.

These examples illustrate the dilemma in building sustainability into the economy. Most laws and regulations pertaining to products and services, while arguably effective, reflect accepted good practice levels. These are not the best practices normally or the leadership levels of products or services (which by definition constitute only a minority of the market), but what is commonly considered baseline or the floor. Such requirements thus typically exclude mediocre or poor performance, the relatively few bad actors as generally recognized by the marketplace, rather than promoting the leaders. Moreover, we have seen that the marketplace needs to undergo a transformation to consider a whole new set of factors in regard to health and environment, so that even good practice and acceptable baselines have to be redefined in light of the sustainability dimension. Therefore, we can expect that laws and regulations incorporating sustainability requirements will generally not be too far-reaching at first. The New York State green cleaning products law for schools, and others like it that followed, are shining exceptions.[13] More typically lawmakers and regulators avoid purchasing or supply requirements that can seriously disadvantage the majority of companies or products in a market.

That is where voluntary programs have been useful and even critical in creating the green economy. Typically these programs do promote leadership products and services; they do

---

13   At the federal level the controversial law to phase out incandescent light bulbs is another exception.

make implicit judgments in favor of one product over another; and they do enhance the business prospects of producers recognized by these programs. They are designed to transform a given market by leveraging the success of the best sustainability performers and thereby encourage lower-level performers to emulate the leaders, thus raising the entire sustainability level of the sector. These voluntary programs escape the negative aspects of mandates by only rewarding, not impugning or prohibiting. They call out the winners, not the losers. They are market-incentive programs that encourage more sustainable production and consumption.

The Promise and Limits of Ecolabeling

Foremost among these voluntary sustainability programs are third-party certification programs, otherwise known as ecolabeling programs. Their functional principles seem straightforward. They set leadership sustainability standards for various categories of products and services, and they award their seal or certification mark to those products or services that are submitted for evaluation and determined to meet the applicable standards. Consumers or institutional purchasers (depending on the product, service, or market) can then identify the product or service as preferable and purchase it. Over time the certified products and services should realize increased sales and market share, and others in their category will strive to achieve certification by reformulation or redesign.

This transformation has actually occurred in a number of markets in dozens of countries around the world where ecolabeling programs have been active. In these cases the market penetration of certified products or services has reached a significant level, in that a substantial minority of products or services has been certified as meeting the ecolabeling standard and other products or services in the category are striving to get certified to reap the sales benefits. As a result, the program has definitely lowered the environmental and health impacts of the category. Even so, in order to avoid stagnation and maintain leadership levels, programs must upgrade their standards periodically so they still capture only the leading products or services in regard to sustainability. If certification becomes commonplace, commoditized, and achievable by all but the lowest sustainability performers, it loses its meaning and leverage.

The building maintenance sector in the United States, particularly janitorial maintenance, illustrates well the market transformation that ecolabeling can achieve. Over the first half-dozen years of this century Green Seal's standard for cleaning products, GS-37, became the *de facto* national green standard in the industry. This came about due to the leadership of several small and large companies, some institutional purchasers such as the US Army and Massachusetts, and even the industry trade association (ISSA).[14] Consequently, many major suppliers of janitorial products have product lines certified to this standard, and it has been specified in numerous procurement bids, policies, and laws, resulting in an overall improvement in the environmental profile of this market sector. To maintain GS-37's leadership levels, Green Seal revised and upgraded the standard in 2007-8.

On the other side, most ecolabeling programs suffer from being unable to penetrate the market to any significant degree in certain categories. Manufacturers or consumers may have

---

14   ISSA did not necessarily promote GS-37 as much as green cleaning as a
      whole.

little interest in a green label; the cost of certification may be too high for the market to bear; or there may be technical challenges for many producers in meeting a leadership level. Often the lack of penetration—and, conversely, the success of an ecolabel in a particular sector—hinges on whether there is a market driver for it. As a voluntary program, ecolabeling has nothing compelling its adoption. It originated on the assumption that consumers were becoming environmentally conscious and would demand green products. Since sustained consumer demand has not yet materialized, green certification depends on other market forces. We saw that a leading state, Massachusetts, was able to drive green product standards in the cleaning products sector through its own purchasing. An even more effective driver occurs when a government body *requires* through legislation or regulation compliance with a *voluntary* ecolabeling standard, as in the case of New York State and its schools. This hybrid is a legitimate result of various market forces at play, however much it causes industry dismay by mandating what was previously discretionary.

To date, then, ecolabeling programs have been an important, useful, but limited tool in constructing the green economy. They could conceivably become a breakthrough force if consumers and purchasers were to embrace them in enough markets. But there are some inherent limitations in ecolabeling, as well, that would need to be overcome.

Certification is necessarily based on standards, and standards, if developed in an open and transparent process and based on multiple attributes, can be highly time-consuming and resource-intensive to produce. One to two years per major product or service category is not unusual for creation (or revision) of such a leadership sustainability standard. Several staff have to be dedicated to such a project, researching the product or service life-cycle impacts, identifying what is available on the market, and dealing with sometimes hundreds of stakeholders interested in participating in the development (or revision) of the standard. For instance, the revision of Green Seal's GS-37 standard took twenty-one months, involved 399 stakeholders, and required several hundred thousand dollars in staff and consultant resources. As a result, even ecolabeling programs in existence for twenty or more years may have in their portfolio only several dozen major standards covering several hundred categories of products and services. In contrast, a major retailer can offer for sale tens of thousands of SKUs.[15]

Developing enough leadership sustainability standards may be the Achilles heel of ecolabeling,[16] but there are other innate challenges that also arise on the certification end. Proper evaluation of a product or service to determine if it meets a standard requires considerable staff time and an audit of the manufacturing or facility site. Typically, the desk evaluation of a product or service submitted for certification itself takes four to six months, given all the data that need to be collected and reviewed (sometimes from suppliers or their suppliers) and the various criteria that need to be analyzed. In addition, every credible certification of a product or service must include an actual inspection of the manufacturing site or service facility in order to determine actual compliance with criteria in the

---

15 Stock-Keeping Unit, the designation warehouses and retailers give to each unique product for sale. In actuality, since each packaged version, style, or variation of a product has a different SKU, the comparison somewhat overstates the discrepancy between coverage of ecolabeling standards and product categories for sale; that is, any given ecolabeling standard may cover many SKUs. But the gap between the two is still significant and daunting.

16 A program officer of the MacArthur Foundation made this observation in a personal communication in the late 1990s.

formulation or design of a product or in the many aspects of operating a service.

These all add up in the time devoted on both sides to the certification process as well as in the fee the ecolabeling program must charge for certification, which also includes the license to use the certification mark (if awarded) and the value of the mark in the market. While ecolabeling programs may graduate their fees depending on the size of the applicant, charging less for small and medium businesses, the fee for certification can still be several thousands of dollars per product or service. The total cost in fees may become significant as a particular producer gets more of its products or services certified.[17]

Given its potential but also its limitations, ecolabeling can be a cornerstone of the green economy, but it will not currently suffice to build the edifice. It correctly focuses on producers and directs them to do things the right way. But it depends also on other responsible parties in the marketplace to create demand for sustainable products and services that producers will heed. Such demand has begun to form, but it is tepid, inconsistent, and inchoate. Several other considerations traditionally have priority over sustainability for institutional purchasers, while consumers experience a variety of competing needs and concerns that are not always aligned with sustainability, as we will see next.

---

17 The cost of certification is an issue frequently raised by industry, but it is often a red herring for lack of interest or market demand. The issue is real, however, for small producers, especially when they want entire product lines certified, and for nearly everyone in a recessionary economy.

CHAPTER 4

Common Consumer Concerns

···

L et us take a brief look at the concerns that drive consumer behavior and purchasing in today's world and compare these to the kinds of values I believe must ultimately save us and our environment. This will be more in the form of a thought survey than a marketing survey of consumer opinions and behavior, but it is based on exposure to decades of such marketing surveys and references to a few recent ones.

While producers are the primary movers for making the economy more sustainable, they are motivated largely by demand from their customers—institutional purchasers or retail consumers, as the case may be. But demand from customers for more sustainable products and services is still sporadic and weak overall, particularly in the retail space, which constitutes seventy percent of the economy. The values consumers reveal through their actual behavior and purchasing do not strongly reflect concern for the common good, much less the world around them. Yet when asked about these broader values consumers invariably claim to be concerned and willing to reduce their impact. This gap between a professed sense of responsibility for society and the environment and the actuality of their behavior—in short, between what they say and what they do—is a key finding of almost every survey of consumer environmental behavior for more than twenty years.

Here are a couple of recent surveys that corroborate this perennial gap in consumer behavior. The Natural Marketing Institute, which has tracked consumer attitudes toward the environment for over a decade, reported in March 2013 that "eighty percent of all Americans are eager to safeguard the future of their health and that of the environment and society around them."[18] (This is the same figure Green Seal obtained in the early 1990s in regard to consumers' interest in buying green products.) In an Earth Day 2013 article summarizing recent surveys of American consumers' attitudes toward the environment, however, Greenbiz.com reported that the latest Cone Communications Green Gap Trend Tracker found a discrepancy between consumers' "action" and "intent." While a record-high seventy-one percent of Americans claim to consider the environment and environmental information in purchasing, less than half say they use or dispose of products in a way that achieves the intended environmental benefit.[19]

Even more to the point, the Green Gauge Survey conducted most recently in 2011 found that "[c]onsumers are more

18 "A Look at Key Sustainability Trends in the United States," Natural Marketing Institute (NMI), March 7, 2013.

19 "Earth Day and the Polling of America, 2013," in GreenBuzz Daily, April 22, 2013.

interested in the convenience many products provide than in the effect they have on the environment." Consumers, in fact, consider their unwillingness to "sacrifice" for environmental protection (including paying more for green products) to be the primary cause of environmental problems. Moreover, due to the recent recession almost half of consumers surveyed feel that other, mainly economic, issues are more important than the environment. Finally, the survey found that only twenty-nine percent of Americans say they buy green products (defined here merely as "made from or packaged in recycled materials").[20]

What, then, are the actual priorities, preoccupations, and values of today's consumer? How important are these, and how do they relate to broader values concerning the welfare of society and the planet? Finally, are the two kinds of values and concerns compatible? Is there hope for some type of alignment between them through a deeper value perspective?

We will first discuss more general consumer concerns then look at specific concerns that come to the fore in actual purchasing of most goods and services.

General Consumer Concerns

Basic Needs. At the most fundamental level we must all take care of basic needs allowing us to survive and to live with at least a moderate level of creature comfort and security. These involve the stuff of everyday purchases and living, including food, personal care, shelter, and mobility (transportation). The essential aspect of these items is largely masked in more affluent societies, where provision of food, shelter, and other necessities is generally assured. But where their supply is threatened or

---

20 *The Environment: Public Attitudes and Individual Behavior—A Twenty-Year Evolution,* GfK (Roper), Green Gauge Survey, 2011.

suddenly diminished, our true need—and nature—comes out. Approaching storms clear the supermarket shelves of what people consider the true necessities (bread, milk, and toilet paper, apparently). Housing shortages prompt people to make unreasonable and ever increasing bids. And broken-down transportation creates temporary havoc and frustrated masses. Depending on the severity of the shortage and its duration, people will act more or less desperately and selfishly to fulfill these needs. Typically in the developed world, though, these basic survival concerns are fulfilled in a mundane way, and the aspect of necessity does not rise to a conscious, much less intense, concern.

Nonetheless, these basic needs must be recognized as fundamental to consumer behavior, and they are perfectly acceptable and natural. All animals exhibit the drive to fulfill these needs, and humans cannot be denied theirs. Of course, our far more extensive technology enables us to have much more of an impact on the earth in fulfilling these needs. Rare are the animals that even come close to the landscape or ecological changes wrought by humans. Also, extraneous motives like profit or other market forces have environmental impacts not directly tied to fulfilling basic needs.

These basic needs generally supersede any greater concern for the world around us, including other people or the environment. A hungry person cares not whether the food is sustainably produced; those needing fire to cook meals and stay warm may cut forests indiscriminately; and in an emergency people choose the surest form of transportation, not the most efficient. When people's basic needs are not satisfied, it would be unreasonable to expect them to consider other more abstract or altruistic objectives. Yet human nature at its best does rise above mere satisfaction of one's own basic needs to consider the needs of others. We just have to make the conceptual jump to realize that other people and species have similar survival needs to our own.[21] So there is, indeed, a potential complementarity between basic needs and broader concerns, provided the former are satisfied.

Health.[22] Closely allied to basic survival and living needs is concern for the health of oneself, family, and friends. Health lurks under the surface of everyday activities and purchases. The healthfulness of our food, personal-care products, and infrastructure is generally taken for granted, and consumers do not generally consider the health impact of their purchases. Yet concern for health can explode when it is compromised. Incidents of contamination in the food supply or of toxins in cosmetics can jar our complacency, while deeper investigation often reveals that our life-support systems are nowhere near as healthy as we presume.[23] So while few people worry about their health in terms of day-to-day activities and purchases, it is a powerful concern that cannot be neglected.

In fact, health has arisen in recent years as a key consumer issue, and it is often the driver for demand for greener products

---

21 The human species may be unique in considering the basic needs of other species, although we do so mostly to satisfy our own or to repair the damage we cause. Other species certainly have symbiotic relationships, and some even display inter-specific rescue behavior, such as dolphins saving a drowning person. But the broader concern appears to be uniquely human.

22 Arguably, health does not belong in this chapter focusing on concerns other than sustainability, as the latter does include consideration of environmental factors (natural or human) that affect human health. But health is also a significant concern in itself that may have no relation to broader considerations of sustainability.

23 For example, much has been written recently about the unhealthy food supply in Western countries, including overuse of antibiotics in livestock, contamination of seafood, use of artificial ingredients like high-fructose corn syrup, and the prevalence of lower-quality fast food (not to mention the even more controversial issue of genetically modified organisms).

and services. Just how safe are the cleaning products we use in our homes or the paints we apply inside and out or the many personal-care products we apply to our bodies daily? The movement for natural or homemade products that grew up in the 1980s has evolved into many Web sites listing greener products and niche companies that provide them. Almost all of these appeal to health. While one may question whether many of these products are actually healthier[24] (or even functionally effective), the concern behind this movement is justified. Thousands of industrial chemicals have been created and employed in the post-World War II economy; yet few have been extensively tested for their health effects. The standards Green Seal and other ecolabeling programs have developed for personal-care, cleaning, and paint products demonstrate that there remain many chemicals in conventional products that can be harmful to human health (as well as the environment).

Health concerns dovetail nicely with broader societal and global concerns. After all, many environmental impacts have human health impacts (e.g., air and water pollution), and others have health impacts on other species (e.g., aquatic toxicity). So concern about one's health can certainly lead to concern about the state of the environment.[25] Moreover, it is not a big

24 One must particularly be cautious about so-called "natural" products. There is no accepted definition of what is natural. Moreover, not everything found in nature is necessarily healthy or safe for humans.

25 In many respects, health concerns have driven the modern environmental movement (1960s on). Incidents of air, water, and hazardous waste pollution helped trigger the fundamental environmental protection laws—Clean Air Act, Clean Water Act, and Superfund. The toxics control law (TSCA) specifically considers human health as well as environmental impact. Even our governmental institutions dedicated to environmental protection, such as the US Environmental Protection Agency, have from the beginning included human health as well as the environment in their mission.

It is interesting to note the complex integration of human health (often referred to as "environmental health" in this context) and environment in the modern environmental movement. This contrasts with the impetus behind

conceptual leap to go from individual and family health to public health and the health of the planet. This does not, however, mean that most people make this connection nor that they do so in their everyday lives and purchasing. As mentioned previously, consumers do not generally connect their purchasing with health impacts. When they do, health tends to be an emotional issue that reflects primarily people's concern about themselves and their loved ones.

Affordability. Another basic concern of consumers is economic. What kind of lifestyle and associated products and services can they afford? For the prudent consumer, the concern here is living within one's means. Of course, many of us are not—or not always —prudent consumers, so we may not apply this measure regularly or rigorously enough in our lives. But by and large everyone has to operate within limits defined by their personal resources.

Affordability affects the whole range of consumer activities and purchases, including the necessities of food, shelter, and transportation. The variety of supermarkets and restaurants and the range of prices in each; house size, style, and location; and modes of transportation (public versus private and variations within each) all reflect choices based to a large degree on affordability. Even health concerns must usually be tailored to affordability. Organic food[26] is perceived as healthier, but it can be considerably more expensive. Safer, better built vehicles are generally more expensive. And housing prices typically reflect

---

the conservation movement in the late 19th and early 20th centuries, which was driven by natural resource depletion. The difference stems both from the uncontrolled plunder of resources in the earlier era as well as the growth of synthetic chemicals in commerce after World War II.

26 Organic food may have both health and environmental benefits, so examples here may reference either or both of these.

locational advantages that include safer neighborhoods or less polluted areas.

Affordability is certainly a legitimate and necessary concern. Our entire free-market system with differential pricing and incomes depends on people generally making choices within their means. As such, affordability is self-regulating. Anyone who ignores it goes bankrupt and drops out of the economic system, or else (in the converse) their hoarded wealth is distributed to their beneficiaries (who generally spend it). While price is an imperfect measure of true societal cost or availability,[27] it does generally succeed in sorting out who can afford what kind of product or service and thus in distributing goods and services throughout society. In the modern marketplace consumers are bombarded with advertising to lure them into purchasing many products and services they may not need or can even afford, and recently credit has been extended too loosely for purchases large and small. But ultimately each consumer must heed the price tag or at least the monthly credit card bill.

Curiously, the notion of individual affordability has an exact parallel with broader societal values related to our environmental impact. The so-called carrying capacity of the earth is the global human population that can live sustainably, considering available food and resources. For society the concept of affordability thus relates directly to the earth's resources and capacity to withstand the stress of human activities and needs. In short, we cannot afford to consume more than the earth can provide, but in fact we are doing just that in the developed countries.

---

27 This is especially true in regard to natural resources and so-called ecosystem services such as clean air and water. Government subsidies such as for fossil fuel production or roads; externalities such as pollution from extraction, manufacturing, use, or disposal; and market factors such as scale and demand can distort price so it does not truly reflect the cost to society to provide a product or service.

Unfortunately, even though personal affordability is a pervasive concern of consumers, it does not automatically lead them to consider whether society (or the earth) can afford their standard of living. While the two concepts are similar in kind, consumers rarely consider the environmental impact of their lifestyle or purchasing, much less society's overall impact on the earth. But because they are used to thinking about affordability, this linkage should be achievable—once consumers' concerns expand beyond themselves.

Individual Welfare. After their basic needs and health concerns are satisfied within the limits of affordability, consumers tend to think about enhancing their well-being through their lifestyle and purchases. Everyone seeks to live well and comfortably. Most people in developed countries have the opportunity to achieve this state for themselves and their families. It is not without hazards, scares, and calamities; but civilization has certainly improved most material aspects of existence.

As society develops materialistically, the line between basic needs and welfare blurs. Ask an average person in an impoverished country what that person really needs, and the answer will be much more basic than what their counterpart in an affluent society says. We know that as our material needs are satisfied and enhanced, our expectations grow accordingly, so that what used to be discretionary or even luxury becomes perceived as necessary. Colloquially, we refer to this as the difference between "needs" and "wants," where the latter are more discretionary. Growing affluence in a society makes the variable nature of "wants" graphic, as we see, for example, how houses or automobiles change over time so that "McMansions" and air-conditioning become standard features when once they were considered luxuries.

The drive for greater individual welfare cannot be underestimated in today's world. It is one of the most significant consumer concerns in developed countries. Advertising plays highly on this concern by enticing people to upgrade their lifestyle and self-image with ever greater material possessions and enhancements. One of the best tricks of advertising is to convince consumers that something they might have perceived as a luxury is really necessary for their lifestyle. A half-century ago the economist John Kenneth Galbraith showed how modern corporations create such demand on the part of consumers through pervasive advertising, so that the traditional notion of supply and demand no longer operates as in a classic free market.

Most of us recognize that this drive for greater individual welfare has gotten out of hand. Certainly, striving for a reasonably comfortable life is natural, and it is part of the culture of Western developed countries, particularly the United States, where everyone wants to enhance their standard of living. But the ferocity of our growing materialism as well as the aberrations it has created (such as disparity of incomes, industrialized agriculture, rampant development, continued environmental degradation, and overstressed lives) have led to a growing movement to question prosperity for its own sake. This counter-movement is manifested in such trends as holistic health, slow food, telework, and community-based economies.

The concern for improving individual welfare has both a negative and a positive relationship to broader concerns for social and planetary welfare. Greater affluence generally means greater consumption, which stresses the environment. While growing affluence can improve the living standard for most classes in society, the gap between rich and poor has grown. On the other hand, historically the impetus for considering societal and planetary welfare has come from the more affluent in society—precisely those who have benefitted from the focus on individual welfare. Moreover, as more people in developed countries gain a higher level of well-being, they should become more sensitized to broader concerns and particularly to their vulnerability if social and environmental systems collapse.

Hence, while the concern for individual welfare is not incompatible with broader and deeper concerns, the connection cannot be assumed and does not happen automatically. And because this consumer concern is so linked to environmental degradation, the drive for individual welfare must be tamed in order to fulfill a broader mission of societal and environmental welfare.

Status. Finally, in the developed countries consumers evaluate their lifestyle and material comfort largely in terms of their peers or those they emulate. Individual welfare becomes defined by the welfare of those with whom one compares oneself. This social comparison leads to the well-known phenomenon of "keeping up with the Joneses," which explains much consumer behavior and purchasing and which seems to operate in most demographic groups above the poverty line. The modern economy exploits social status concerns quietly but ruthlessly, from personal care and appearance to houses to virtually every other aspect of lifestyle.

Concern for status can be almost as strong a driver as basic needs. Looking at typical consumer behavior today, one could well believe that status is a paramount concern for many, so desperately do they strive to fulfill it. In the throes of this concern, not much else may seem important, until basic needs are threatened. Some even go so far as to compromise their basic needs by ignoring affordability in their quest to achieve status. The resulting individual bankruptcy or destitution is, unfortunately, a not uncommon story for those aspiring to a higher status.

Given its strength as a consumer concern, status poses special challenges in trying to move society to deeper, more altruistic concerns. While spiritual leaders might decry status as a vice, it remains a significant factor in the modern economy. The need for constant economic growth almost requires the continuous social comparison that fuels ever more purchasing at ever higher levels. So until we refashion our economy in terms of more enduring values than growth, status concerns will remain significant if not actually worthwhile. People will continue to strive to match their peers and those above in terms of their material welfare and lifestyle.

There is a way out, however. The recent movement of "gamification"—using goals, achievement levels, and reward systems in areas where they have not traditionally been used—is being applied to sustainability concerns in many areas of business and individual life. Gamification harnesses this drive to compete and attain a higher level of status, and sustainability goals can substitute for more materialistic ones still within the context of a competitive game. Utilities are discovering that they can induce consumers to reduce their energy use most effectively by giving them real-time comparisons to their neighbors. Businesses are adopting gamification programs to induce greener employee behavior in the form of point systems, leader boards, and awards. In a sense the whole movement of ecolabeling is a form of gamification, as brought home to me touchingly by the mechanic who rushed over to me during the audit of a postal service vehicle maintenance facility to ask, "Did we get the Green Seal?" By redirecting social comparison to the values we know are more important and lasting, the urge for status can ultimately be tapped for the good of society and the planet.

Specific Consumer Concerns

Consumers are thus motivated by general concerns involving basic needs, health, affordability, individual welfare, and status. These concerns inform and shape all consumer behavior and purchasing. They also underlie the specific (and more concrete) concerns that come into play in actual purchases of goods and services, which we look at now.

The specific concerns of consumers when making a particular purchase include the following: need/want, health/safety, cost, quality/performance, status/style, and brand/loyalty. Not all of these may be involved in any given purchase, and the degree of importance of each will vary depending on the individual and the individual purchase. Several of these derive directly from the general concerns and do not require much more elaboration. As before, our central interest is the disparity between these concerns and deeper societal concerns such as sustainability, and more specifically how typical purchasing concerns relate to buying greener products and services.

Need/Want. This concern combines basic needs, individual welfare, and status. The line between "need" and "want" can be a very individual decision relating to a consumer's social context, self-image, and aspirations. Where status plays an important role in a purchase, such as for a house, the "want" can be predominant. As such, the consumer may be unwilling to consider other concerns such as sustainability, especially if the latter are perceived as compromising higher welfare or status.[28]

---

28   Of course, concern for sustainability does not necessarily require other values to be compromised, but it is often perceived as doing so. Sometimes

If a purchase is truly in the category of a legitimate need, fulfilling the need remains paramount. Broader concerns can be considered, but again only if they do not interfere with fulfilling the need. If the basic need is intense, other concerns will be disregarded. More likely in an affluent society, consumers can consider layering deeper values on their basic needs. A car is a necessity for most American families; yet a consumer may opt for a more fuel-efficient one. Likewise, a person may choose to buy food that is certified to be sustainably produced, thus fulfilling both their own needs and higher societal ones. As we have seen, however, most consumers do not think about the latter when satisfying their basic needs.

Health/Safety. Few consumers consciously consider health and safety when making a purchase unless an issue has arisen in the market with regard to a particular product, ingredient, or service. In such cases the opportunity arises to move the market toward greener alternatives. Examples include the rise of low- or no-VOC (volatile organic compound) paints, restrictions on plasticizers (potential endocrine disruptors) in toys, and removal of high-fructose corn syrup from some foods. Such specific health concerns can also provide the leverage for considering other health and environmental issues in regard to these and other products, as consumers become more sensitized to (or suspicious of) a product's potential impacts.

The few consumers who do consider health and safety in their everyday purchases face enormous challenges in finding and interpreting the relevant information. Ecolabeling programs such as Green Seal are designed to do this job for the consumer. They provide the necessary analysis of health and environmental

---

the greener choice actually carries higher status and is not perceived as a compromise at all; hybrid cars have gained market traction in this way.

data and signal with a seal on a product that it is healthier and more sustainable than most. Where such certified products do not exist in a category, consumers are generally at a loss[29] and have to rely on products and brands that proclaim their greenness or retailers that specialize in such products.

Cost. For most of us, price is a central concern in almost any purchase, and it relates directly to the general concern for affordability. In virtually every category of product and service we buy—from food to houses to transportation to vacations—we stratify the offerings according to our means. Nonetheless, we may be somewhat flexible on the purchase cost if we can attain some other values, such as greater quality, status, or brand.

Cost is often raised as a red flag in green purchasing, but it is as often a red herring. Yes, certain greener products and services can cost more, but they may do so only for the initial, not life-cycle, cost.[30] In a number of markets greener products have actually attained cost parity with conventional ones. Until the market completely transitions to greener products and services, it may still reflect differential pricing due to subsidies (such as for fossil fuel development), economies of scale (disadvantageous for greener, still niche products), and externalities (not accounted for in conventional products). That is why governments and utilities offer rebates or credits from time to time for greener

---

29   The nascent movement to require disclosure of complete product information (so-called radical transparency) may promise more than it can deliver, both because of necessary trade secrets and because of the difficulty of interpreting such complex information.

30   As touched on in the previous chapter, the life-cycle cost of a product or service considers not only initial purchase cost but also the cost of operation and maintenance over its lifetime. Thus, for example, a more efficient and durable appliance may well pay back over its (longer) lifetime the higher initial cost compared to a conventional one. A consumer should likewise beware of houses nicely priced because developers install cheaper, less efficient appliances and heating and air-conditioning systems; the homeowner will be paying back for years to come in higher operating costs.

products that cost more. Consumers must realize that healthier, more efficient, and more durable products may sometimes have to cost more,[31] but they will have benefits in the long run that cannot always be quantified, as in the case of health.

Where life-cycle costs are lower, consideration of cost in a purchase nicely complements sustainability concerns. To the extent cost reflects true societal and environmental cost, choosing the product or service with lower life-cycle cost reduces the burden on society and the planet as well as on the individual. For example, energy-efficient lamps, such as CFLs or LEDs,[32] typically cost more upfront per unit. But they last much longer and burn at much lower wattage than conventional incandescent lamps. Hence, a simple calculation demonstrates that their life-cycle cost is, in fact, significantly lower, and smart consumers will benefit both themselves and the planet by purchasing them, despite the steeper initial price tag.[33]

The problem in our transitional economy occurs where the market cost for the more sustainable product significantly exceeds that of the more environmentally impactful product, even over the life cycle. Consumers then face the dilemma of

---

31   In this regard, the drive to lower prices on consumer goods, a contemporary market phenomenon brought about by the big-box retail stores, could have a perverse effect on sustainability. Suppliers can be squeezed only so much without compromising on the quality of their materials or the wages and conditions of their workers. It will be interesting to see how Walmart, the pioneer in such retail marketing, will be able to balance its low-price mantra with its more recent conversion and commitment to sustainability.

32   Compact fluorescent lamps and light-emitting diodes.

33   Some environmental life-cycle impacts demonstrate similar paradoxes. When Green Seal developed its standard for CFLs (GS-5), it not only showed that life-cycle costs for them are lower, but also that the overall amount of mercury in the lamp life cycle is reduced, despite its presence in CFLs and not in incandescent bulbs. This can be derived by considering the trace amounts of mercury in coal, which is the predominant fuel for generating electricity in most of the United States, and the much greater energy required in using incandescent bulbs.

incurring greater personal cost for the sake of greater global good. This is often the case with organic food or durable goods, and all but the zealous may balk at paying prices so highly marked up. So cost can be a real barrier to higher values, where such a differential occurs.

Quality/Performance. No one intentionally buys a product or service that doesn't do its job. That just results in wasted money, time, and materials, or worse. The same applies to the green economy. Standards for greener products and services, such as those developed by ecolabeling programs, must include functional performance criteria to ensure these products and services do the job as well as conventional alternatives.

Unfortunately, greener products have been tainted with the reputation of not working very well or requiring much more effort to work than conventional products. This perception took hold in the 1980s with the advent of greener products in the marketplace, when many of them were, indeed, inferior in functional performance.[34] Institutional purchasers and consumers alike still harbor some doubts and prejudices against greener products, and truly there remain a few that warrant this disrepute.

But as the green market has matured over the past several decades, manufacturers of greener products have worked hard to ensure they are functionally comparable to conventional products.[35] So consumers should not be leery of switching

---

34 Some of the most egregious examples included compact fluorescent lamps that made people look green; recycled copy paper that jammed machines; paint without proper hiding power; recycled tissue that was brown and rough; and auto dish detergent that left copious films, spots, and even food on wares.

35 In the evolution of product formulation and design to include environmental and health considerations, certain potent but potentially harmful ingredients have been removed from all products on the market today. No one would argue that a cleaning product based on benzene or other petroleum distillates—commonly used a generation ago—is not more "effective" than

to greener alternatives for fear of inadequate performance, especially if they are independently certified to standards that include functional performance. The growing number of greener products in the consumer market, especially from mainstream companies and name brands, indicates that consumers are overcoming this concern and are therefore open to considering quality and performance in greener terms.

Status/Style. In the developed countries, and especially in the United States, virtually any purchase can trigger a concern about status and style. From the most basic purchase of food or clothing to the grandest, such as a house or car, status and style can figure more or less in determining a consumer's choice and can actually dominate a consumer's decision.

As discussed earlier, concern for status and style can be harnessed to higher purposes through such techniques as gamification. For the green economy to work overall, however, greener products and services have to be perceived as smarter, cooler, and more desirable. We need to have many "counter-SUVs"—vehicles and virtually everything else that are greener choices but which catch on with consumers as quickly as sports utility vehicles did. (Hybrid cars have shown some of this potential, but their much greater cost limits their uptake.) Only when consumers embrace deeper concerns for sustainability and demand greener products throughout the economy is this likely to occur.

---

contemporary products without such ingredients; but having significant amounts of carcinogens in a product is no longer acceptable. In only a few instances, to our knowledge, have greener products not measured up to their contemporary counterparts, such as floor finishes with cross-linking agents other than zinc (which is toxic to aquatic life) when used in high-volume areas such as retail store entrances (zinc-free finishes work well everywhere else). In the home, greener products may require some more mechanical effort or time, but not so much as to make them inferior in performance, or the product has failed in its purpose and should be replaced.

Brand/Loyalty. In specific purchases most consumers consider the particular brand of a product or service, and many show loyalty to a brand or to the company behind it. Often, this brand preference and loyalty stem from all the other concerns, in that a brand or company has previously supplied goods the consumer considers to work well, be reasonably priced, fulfill their needs, and fit their sense of status or style.

Yet the rise of private-labeled products in retail stores suggests that preference for brand is not inelastic, especially in regard to cost. Brand is also highly vulnerable to reputation, and bad publicity or inferior performance can besmirch a brand or company's reputation permanently. Hence, the concern for brand can work two ways in transitioning to a green economy: it may pose an obstacle in replacing traditional, branded products with greener ones; or it may catalyze the movement to greener brands as consumer priorities change in their favor.

....

Truly, many other consumer concerns potentially crowd out broader, deeper societal values for sustainability. These competing values operate both at a general level of consumer consciousness and, perhaps even more intensely, at the time of specific purchases. The good news about this values mix is that most of these other concerns are not necessarily incompatible with sustainability concerns. As we have seen, with a shift in values, they can be quite consistent, as with health and affordability.

The values gap that keeps the economy and all of us as consumers from functioning more sustainably stems fundamentally from our view of the world around us. As long as we do not see that world as central to our lives and to everything we do, the gap will persist. As long as the environment, environmental health, and nature are seen as just another "issue" in the political and cultural spectrum, we will fail to subsume ordinary consumer concerns within a more meaningful and durable framework. The greening of the economy will proceed at its current inadequate pace; we will continue to degrade the environment and our life support; and the future of life on earth will become uncertain. We need to find a connection at a deeper level that will catalyze all of society to act more responsibly and sustainably, so we may consummate the culture change that has begun—while there is still time.

CHAPTER 5

Our Moral Relationship with Nature

....

Our relationship to nature is essentially a moral one. Our destruction of the environment is potential suicide not only because we would be destroying our material life support, but, more disturbingly, because we would be violating the aesthetic, moral, and spiritual values that are intrinsic to human character.

If the greening of the economy over the past few decades has not yet staved off environmental disaster, we need to look more deeply at our relationship to our world and our attitude toward nature for a root cause and solution. The still prevailing attitude toward our environment's degradation can best be characterized as a mixture of ignorance and disregard. Yet there are two critical and compelling reasons for caring about the environment and its degradation, both related to human survival.

One reason is relatively straightforward and well-documented, although still not widely understood or appreciated: that the very survival of humanity in *physical* terms depends on an intact, functioning environment that provides us with basic life support and sustenance. The other reason, ultimately as or more important, goes to the heart of what we consider most human and humane—the *moral* values that define us, and which our relationship to nature both shapes and reflects.

Human dependence on nature for basic physical survival can easily be forgotten in today's highly urbanized and technological world. It isn't merely a joke that many children—not just inner city ones—grow up thinking their food is produced at a supermarket. Our love of machines and of our technical abilities has only increased through the industrial and high-tech revolutions; most of us prefer to marvel over snazzy automobiles than beautiful landscapes, and our young people are usually too absorbed in their digital devices to look at the world around them. Nature has been so tamed and cultivated for the most part that we treat its outbreaks in storms, earthquakes, and other natural disasters as unwarranted intrusions on our lives. And we have so successfully harnessed for human consumption nature's productivity from both plants and animals that we assume these natural and cultivated systems are invulnerable and perpetual.

Recall or recognize that our food comes from the earth, its land and sea, however much we cultivate or re-engineer its habitats and species.[36] Recall or recognize that our water comes

---

36   Artificial cultivation only highlights the extent to which the earth naturally provides bounteous nutrients in many forms in support of agriculture. A greenhouse, for example, artificially protects its inhabitants from

from the earth, its land and sea, and that the need to purify its freshwater stems largely from our own pollution of it. Recall or recognize that the air we breathe comes from the earth's atmosphere, that oh-so-thin layer that blankets us but gives us life through oxygen, warmth, and protection from radiation and meteors. Recall or recognize that our homes and habitations come from the earth, its forests and minerals, and the land upon which we dwell.

Then recall or recognize that each of these aspects of our earth—its land, sea, freshwater, forests, and minerals—are under stress or being depleted because of human consumption and exploitation. Arable land is diminishing as urban development overtakes farmland. Remaining farmlands are over-cropped, and top soils are eroded. Freshwater is increasingly contaminated, both on the surface and in aquifers, and freshwater supplies are becoming scarcer as populations burgeon. The great oceans increasingly show signs of degradation from pollution, overfishing, and chemical alteration from climate change. The atmosphere, endless though it seems, registers increasing levels of trace gases that are already disrupting our climate and weather patterns. Our forests have been receding at alarming rates, especially in the tropics, due to lumbering and clearing for agriculture, while we dig more deeply, widely, and disruptively to extract minerals from the earth. And the land we inhabit on unstable or marginal areas slides down valleys or gets swamped by the sea. We are eroding and destroying the basic natural

---

temperatures they cannot tolerate, but normally it must be heated, ventilated, or even cooled at considerable cost in fossil fuels, and water must be manually supplied. At the extreme—the experiment ("Biosphere 2") to create an entirely enclosed and self-sufficient ecosystem, replicating the earth—humans not only invested huge amounts of resources in trying to duplicate what the earth does for free, but essentially failed in the attempt.

systems, structures, and functions upon which our lives utterly depend. We should, indeed, care.

But we must not stop here. It is entirely natural to care about our own survival and to value our environment in terms of human sustenance and survival. Self-preservation is both primordial and essential, and no one should begrudge humanity—or, for that matter, any other species—for taking what it needs from nature for its reasonable maintenance and perpetuation. But this implicit license for the living does not extend to wantonly destroying other species or their habitats, and it is completely counter-productive when it involves undermining our own life support. Moreover, apart from the obviously suicidal aspect of such behavior, it denies an entire dimension of humanity that is equally essential to our lives— our moral character.

Developing in the Moral Dimension

Caring and showing responsibility for the world beyond ourselves are critical aspects of the moral development of individuals in most human societies. This sense of responsibility, or caring for the welfare of others, must underlie any ethical behavior; otherwise the latter is simply rote adherence to social norms. In truly moral development individuals make a transition from merely satisfying their own immediate needs and wants to considering how they affect others in their lives and can even help and not harm them.

We see this moral development play out graphically in children. An infant begins as a mostly self-absorbed and needy being whose sphere of perception is scarcely arms' length and dominated by basic survival instincts. It may interact with our smiles and touches, but we can be pretty sure it isn't thinking about our needs. Toddlers, children, and often teenagers maintain this predominantly self-centered outlook, but their perception enlarges as they grow so they are at least aware of a greater world around them and the expressed needs of other people. During this time, especially in the teen years, the individual begins to understand that others have needs that should be considered nearly as much as their own, and the individual begins to show some care and sense of responsibility for things external to him or herself. This may begin with a cherished pet or plaything and usually evolves into broader and deeper feelings of concern for other people and creatures.

We call out those who do not make this transition as self-centered, egotistic, or even narcissistic. Such individuals, who fail to develop moral character, do not usually do well in society. At worst, they flout legitimate laws and social conventions, becoming disreputable, criminal, or even sociopathic. At best, they go through life leaving a trail of damage affecting themselves and others, materially or emotionally. They may succeed in their business or profession, but not in their personal lives. They rarely garner respect as human beings.

How we relate to the people and environment around us thus both reflects and forms our moral character. If we are not encouraged early on, usually by parents, to consider the legitimate needs and feelings of others, the moral dimension may have difficulty developing, and we are in danger of becoming morally stunted. Certainly the experience of being told to consider a sibling's feelings or rights (much less those of a friend or stranger) can be disturbing, eye-opening, even deflating; are we not the center of the universe? Continuing life experiences help us assimilate this orientation until it becomes ingrained if not instinctive. We come to value our family, friends, and other loved ones and care about their welfare comparably to our own.[37]

Expanding Our Circle of Care

But the moral dimension must ultimately extend beyond our own circle of family and friends, since they simply become an extension of ourselves. We must apply the same moral principles more broadly, including to strangers and to society at large. This is what our laws and social mores address, although in purely behavioral (and typically punitive) terms. This is also what ethical behavior incorporates and why we disapprove of cheating even when it does not directly affect someone else—it affects others indirectly and undermines social trust. Good moral character does not stop to consider whether the subject under consideration is within its circle of care, but rather responds sincerely to do the right thing for the right internal motive.[38]

Now most of us have a limit on how far we take this other-centeredness. The boundary of genuine care and moral responsibility (cf. ethical behavior) typically gets drawn around family and friends, social groups we are part of or have affinity to, and, under certain circumstances, fellow nationals. Tragic incidents involving people external to these groups

---

37   Appropriate concern about ourselves is also part of moral development
     and maturity; in contrast to immediate gratification, it shows we care about
     our own welfare and integrity in the longer term. This also relates to the
     much-quoted truism that self-love is a precondition for loving others. Self-
     denigration does not make for a very loving or moral individual. In contrast,
     self-sacrifice may well reflect moral character.

38   In the extreme for most of us, the moral individual puts the welfare of others
     above his or her own and may make the ultimate sacrifice of his or her own
     life to save another's. Many have done this and deserve to be remembered,
     but I must single out a relatively recent example in the airplane crash in
     Washington, DC, in 1982, when a bystander jumped into the icy river to save
     lives (he survived) and a passenger kept helping others get lifted out of the
     water instead of himself (he succumbed).

may, of course, invoke our temporary concern; but we will not normally feel much obligation toward them. Xenophobia, or fear of strangers, represents an extreme version of this compartmentalization of care, along with what Erik Erikson termed the "pseudospeciation" of other humans that is expressed in racist attitudes toward groups of skin color unlike our own and false beliefs that they belong to inferior species. It also explains why war is possible and mass murder in war may be accepted or at least justified. Conversely, civil wars act against the ingrained allegiance we have to fellow nationals, and they can be instigated only by differentiating the other side through some other group distinction such as ethnicity, geography, religion, or social class,[39] which ultimately leads to the creation of another nation.

Unfortunately, these limits on our other-centeredness also apply to our relationship to the non-human world, with equally heinous results. We care about our dog and cat, our backyard, and nature in our backyard; but distant lands and wild animals can generally be exploited with little concern or protest. We put our dumps on the edge of town, bordering the next (foreign territory, in this context). The more alien the place or species, the less likely we will show concern about them. Environmental groups justifiably complain about (but also exploit) the difference in how people react to threats affecting "mega-fauna" such as dolphins or pandas compared to insects or mollusks. The former are mammals, like us, and therefore invoke more sympathy as part of our group.

We do get aroused about threats to "postcard" areas such as national parks or similar unspoiled terrain such as tropical

---

39 Or even something as trivial as uniform color, as when Americans fought each other as Union Blue and Confederate Gray. This is not to say there were not much deeper differences between the sides in the US Civil War, but in the heat of battle color probably became the key differentiator and motivator.

rainforest. This is a good thing, or such areas would surely vanish through exploitation.[40] But our natural gems are really the geographic equivalent of mega-fauna. We do not show comparable concern about the much greater area of natural land that is not as photogenic or appealing to humans. Yet the land between the gems and our backyards constitutes the plain but vital matrix of nature upon which ecosystems depend. We cannot isolate ecosystems and expect them to function normally. The conservation strategy to save critical lands and sensitive ecosystems, often based on concentration of endangered species, may be a reasonable response to rapid degradation; but ultimately it may fail because it does not include the connections among lands and ecosystems. This weakness is becoming especially apparent in light of climate change, as the natural corridors for plant and animal migration in response to such change no longer exist or are blocked.

Expanding Our View of Nature

We must see nature as a continuum we live in rather than as something separate and apart from us. As with pollution and the effects of our economy, nature is not something "out there" for which others are responsible, but an intrinsic part of our lives for which we are all stewards. We should be concerned about threats not only to national parks, but also to other natural areas[41] and to species that inhabit or pass through them. Otherwise we are

---

40 Tropical rainforest seems to be disappearing in any case, despite a reasonable amount of concern in the developed world; but without the latter the rate of deforestation would likely be even greater.

41 Land trusts are a good example of such concern. While hundreds of national, regional, and local trusts have actively protected land in the United States, often by conservation easement, the amount of protected land from these trusts remains a small fraction of the total.

limiting our recognition of the effect we as a society have on our natural world and of our collective responsibility for our impacts. Psychologically, the demarcation of nature into valued and expendable areas allows us not to care about the latter, even though this differentiation is somewhat artificial and a form of pseudospeciation.[42,43] Such distinctions also significantly lessen our appreciation and understanding of nature and the world around us because we typically do not pay much attention to more ordinary places.

What arouses people's concern is the subject of intense marketing interest. We know from experience that most middle-class Americans pay attention when their health, or that of their families, is affected by a product, activity, or nearby land use. We live in the legacy of Lucky Strike, Three Mile Island, and Love Canal. In each of these cases there was a direct and substantial threat to people's health and welfare that galvanized concern and even governmental action. Such reaction is to be expected and will continue to be a strong and legitimate factor in the marketplace. But it simply covers the self-centered or group-centered dimension of concern. What about the health and welfare of the greater world outside, including all the other species with whom we co-inhabit the earth?

---

42   Our focus on sensitive and ecologically valuable areas should not be eliminated but rather complemented by concern for the larger area around them. This broader focus has begun to happen in devising management plans for national parks and wilderness areas, and in stewardship and remediation plans for valuable ecosystems. For example, it is now recognized that the Chesapeake Bay cannot be cleaned up or protected without considering land use activities in all the upland areas of its watershed.

43   Speaking of pseudospeciation as applied to nature, some bird-watchers call common birds such as starlings, grackles, and doves "trash birds." Granted, some of these are non-native species that have become over-populated in the United States (through no fault of their own), but they are equally a part of our current ecosystem.

Moral Concern Is Boundless

We have to make this transition, this enlargement of the scope of our concern to the broader world around us, because care for the non-self is not limited morally. We have seen that a necessary part of moral development involves expanding the range of concern to those outside ourselves and our own identity groups. There is no moral reason why this expansion should stop at any point; the scope of caring and of moral concern is potentially boundless. Any boundary, including family, social class, nationality, or race, is an artificial constriction on morality and our moral character. Instead, as individuals and as a society, we must expand our concern and moral framework to an ever broader circle that includes the next family, the next town, the next class, the next nation, and the next race, recognizing that all humanity is one and worthy of identical care and treatment. To do otherwise is to make morality merely a self-serving code of conduct that enhances one group implicitly (or explicitly) at the expense of all others.

This boundlessness of morality applies also to other species and even to inanimate nature. We apply this principle already to domesticated animals in our care, speaking of humane treatment and penalizing those who are cruel to animals. As we have become more secure in our place in nature, we can perceive wild species not just as threats or pests but as living creatures that are worthy in their own right and deserve to be protected.[44] Once we accept responsibility for the care of wild species, protection of

---

44 The US Endangered Species Act was established at least in part because of the growing recognition by humans of the inherent value of wild species. The act states that "fish, wildlife, and plants are of esthetic, ecological, educational, historical, recreational, and scientific value to the nation and its people" and speaks of "the nation's heritage in fish, wildlife, and plants." These values for other species go far beyond the typical consumptive or exploitative uses for subsistence or commercial benefit.

their habitats and ecosystems follows necessarily. We must view the earth's landscapes not just as human habitat and resources but also as habitat for wild species.

Beyond this biological level of concern we must consider even inanimate landforms for their intrinsic value to humans,[45] as intricate and often beautiful features that have evolved through natural processes. No one argues that rocks feel pain as animals do. Humans, though, can be upset by mountaintop mining or the destruction of a special natural feature (e.g., damming of Hetch Hetchy Valley in California) because something of value and beauty in human terms has been lost.[46] As we learn more about the earth's surface processes we also become more sensitive to the changes we impose on landscapes because of their potentially disruptive effect on these complicated, integrated processes.[47]

---

45   The evolution of Western landscape art reflects this growing value for nature itself. Landscape in the Middle Ages and Renaissance served primarily as background for human (religious) scenes. In the seventeenth and eighteenth centuries it became part of a pastoral scene with humans centrally in the picture. But in the nineteenth century it became the subject itself, one of awe, veneration, and beauty, often in grandiose scenes such as portrayed by the Hudson River School and Western US artists.

46   The establishment of national parks in the United States starting in 1872 reflected the insight that certain areas of inanimate nature have a singular value that must be protected. The most visionary of our nature prophets such as Muir and Thoreau often likened these and other wilderness areas to temples or divine places.

     Curiously, national forests became established a few decades later in the United States explicitly for exploitative purposes, but with the intention of conserving resources for the future through forest reserves. Only much later, in the latter twentieth century, did more intrinsic values of forests, such as wilderness and aesthetics, come to compete with commercial uses in sometimes heated battles over specific tracts and overall management approaches.

47   Earth surface processes include: hydrologic, the action and result of water movement; pedologic, the development of soils; aeolian, the action and result of wind; meteorologic, the action and result of weather (e.g., weathering); and geologic, the action and result of earth dynamics on the surface (e.g., lava flows, sedimentation, tectonic movements).

Now the boundlessness of moral concern still allows a hierarchy or relativity of concern, generally out of necessity, that may favor a closer circle of self and identity groups. We expect people to protect themselves and their families and to put these ahead of distant habitats or other species. All species, humans included, are justifiably programmed for self-survival.[48] This moral relativity, however, does not violate or invalidate broader moral concern. The value for other objects (animate or inanimate) beyond one's immediate circle still remains, even if one has to sacrifice them for one's own survival or that of one's loved ones. Native Americans notably venerated the buffalo even as they consumed it (completely) for sustenance. Hence, enlarging the scope of moral concern to virtually anything outside us does not necessarily require self-deprivation or self-sacrifice. In fact, we may refer to the latter as "beyond the call [of duty]" precisely because it is not morally required and may not even be the best course of action.[49]

Addressing Practical Limits through Attitude and Balance

Essentially, the only legitimate boundary to moral concern, if it should be considered that at all, derives from the practical necessity of survival and achievement of well-being. We

---

48 In purely survival mode, which was the experience of Americans in the wilderness until the mid-nineteenth century, it is difficult to consider nature as something to be valued and protected, much less as an object of moral concern. Understandably the movements to protect and value nature noted above came after most of the country had been "tamed."

49 Self-sacrifice may actually lead to greater overall harm when considering the effects on one's closest circle. For example, if the heroes in the airplane crash referenced above had young families, the welfare of several people could have been compromised to save a stranger with unknown dependents. Of course, in an emergency one does not have this information and cannot make this calculus; one's inner values to protect and save others take over.

must protect ourselves and provide for our own sustenance by consuming a portion of nature, including its plants and animals. We may also legitimately strive to attain a reasonably comfortable state of existence above that of mere subsistence.[50] In doing so, we should apply two mitigating factors, attitude and balance, which are key in determining what is appropriate use of the environment versus exploitation of it. Attitude relates to the value we place on all living things and aspects of nature even though we may have to consume a portion of them. We have discussed above the moral basis behind such attitude and its characteristic concern, care, and respect for everything outside ourselves.

Balance relates to how we interact with and consume nature and whether we leave its integrity intact in doing so. With the proper attitude our actions should allow for our own needs and also for those of the world around us. This balance is achieved when we maintain the wholeness and proper functioning (integrity) of nature, specifically the structure and function of ecosystems and landscapes.[51] Human development can be in design with nature and at an appropriate scale in

---

50 Determining what is a reasonable level of comfort is a critical issue in defining a sustainable society today. This is a very complex matter and the subject for another discourse. The point here is that while humans deserve both sustenance and well-being, which may come at the expense of the rest of nature, our taking of nature should have limits, both physical and psychological.

51 This concept is akin to Aldo Leopold's celebrated land ethic: "Quit thinking about decent land-use as solely an economic problem. Examine each question in terms of what is ethically and esthetically right, as well as what is economically expedient. A thing is right when it tends to preserve the integrity, stability, and beauty of the biotic community. It is wrong when it tends otherwise." "The land ethic simply enlarges the boundaries of the community to include soils, waters, plants, and animals, or collectively: the land... [A] land ethic changes the role of *Homo sapiens* from conqueror of the land-community to plain member and citizen of it. It implies respect for his fellow-members and also respect for the community as such" (Aldo Leopold, *A Sand County Almanac* (New York: Oxford University Press, 1989), 204, 224-225).

keeping with nature's systems or the reverse. A building, alpine development, or city can work within the natural processes around it, whereas a coastal community or megalopolis may strain these processes or be out of harmony with them.[52] We know that earth surface processes work together in a more-or-less integrated system, so anything that disrupts them can destroy the landscape's integrity and be out of balance with nature. Soil erosion from clearing, stream diversions and dams, desertification, much less human-induced climate change—all are disruptions of earth processes that significantly affect landscapes and ecosystems.

The interaction of attitude and balance toward the environment plays out every day in our decisions about consumption. Food is a prominent example. Human need for food can be satisfied sustainably by maintaining wild stocks (e.g., fisheries); by low-till agriculture that minimizes soil erosion; by organic practices that do not poison the environment (and leave toxic residues on our food); and by reducing the production of meat, which has such a high toll on resources. In other areas, housing can be supplied through more sustainable materials such as certified wood and renewable energy systems, and our homes can be maintained through non-toxic chemicals, which protect both us and aquatic ecosystems. Our transportation choices can have enormous impacts, and while we cannot escape the use of automobiles in our modern society we can minimize these impacts in many ways—including where we live and work, how we organize our trips, and even how we drive. In all these activities we can be mindful of both our

---

52 Mountaintop mining is a flagrant example of disruption of the landscape that leaves a permanent scar, both in loss of landform and in destruction of aquatic ecosystems through sedimentation.

legitimate needs and the welfare of our world, thus preserving a balance between them.[53]

Relating to Other Animals

Our relationship with wild animal species, in particular, demonstrates the range of our attitudes and behaviors toward nature. On the one side is wanton consumption of animals without concern for preservation of species or individuals. In the most egregious cases, the "consumption" may merely be for "sport," as in the mass killing of buffalo (left on the prairie) in the nineteenth century. Also in this category are trophy hunting, which considers an animal a mere decoration or status symbol, and partial harvesting, as in the taking of shark fins or elephant tusks. Clearly, no thought or concern is given here to the animal or its species, and both may suffer demise as a result.

At the other end of the range we can treasure other species but also be impractically protective of them. It is just not possible to live in this world without consuming, however indirectly, other animals. Every step we take probably extinguishes some small microscopic creatures. Every consumptive activity in the landscape, be it agriculture or housing, will necessarily take some individuals and their habitats. But we can consider these impacts ahead of time and limit our take as much as reasonably possible, applying the proper attitude and balance in our necessary consumption. Those who choose not to take animals

---

53 As we have seen in a previous chapter, however, even the application of proper attitude and balance on the part of individuals may not be sufficient in our present economy to maintain a sustainable world. But if everyone were to behave accordingly, we would be much closer to a sustainable economy and certainly be better positioned—through consumer demand on manufacturers—to achieve it.

as food determine that this kind of consumption is not necessary for them.[54]

Hunting presents complex considerations along this spectrum. In many ecosystems today hunting is necessary to keep populations of browsers like deer in check because their natural predators have been eliminated. Many people grow up with the experience of hunting in their family, and they consider it a sport that combines companionship with immersion in the wilds. For many hunters it is their primary way of connecting with nature and being outdoors. Hunters often use the meat of their prey, even if they also revel in a trophy. Some knowledge of the hunted species is required to be successful, and hunters have to outwit their prey by overcoming the latter's naturally superior senses.

For those who do not hunt, hunting can appear to cross the line between legitimate consumption and unnecessary harm to other species. Most people do not need to hunt to survive, although they may benefit from obtaining their food this way. In terms of ecosystem function, those against hunting generally do not appreciate the need for keeping certain species in check through hunting, and they often decry special hunts organized for this purpose. But the real objection to hunting, the moral reproach, concerns killing an animal as sport—and sometimes not killing it, but wounding it and causing it to suffer until it dies. Certainly most hunters care about proper kills to avoid merely wounding an animal, but this cannot be assured nor the latter always prevented.

---

54 Unfortunately, not everyone who is inclined in this direction can physically follow through with it. Current holistic nutritional theory maintains that some human blood types actually require meat in their diet, based on our ancestral origins as hunters.

Furthermore, one may well wonder how sportsmanlike it is to kill an animal at distant range with rifles and other lethal weapon technologies, however superior animal senses may be over human.

At this time there cannot be a right answer on the complex issue of hunting, especially given its need in wildlife management. The cultural, economic, and demographic differences between hunters and non-hunters must also be acknowledged (one man's meat. . .). But one can envision a time in the future when all the necessities and benefits hunting brings could be satisfied by less lethal means. As wilderness increasingly shrinks due to human development, could we not allow wild species the peace of not being targeted by humans in their own habitats? In a functioning ecosystem most species have enough natural predators to worry about.

In discussions about wildlife one often hears concern for the species and little for the individual. This reflects the prevailing ecological (scientific) emphasis on protection of species. Certainly the welfare of a species as a whole must come first; otherwise there will be no more individuals in it. But often a kind of callousness, devaluing, or at the least disregard for the welfare of individual animals attends the discussion of wild populations, as if the individual animal does not matter at all. No doubt this attitude derives from our historical relationship to other species in the wild, where they were either feared predators or relished prey. But it also stems from the notion that other animals do not have feelings and, short of torture, do not suffer as humans do.

Anyone who has interacted with animals, whether domesticated or not, can attest to their capacity for feelings or at least sensory response.[55,56] Animals may very well be more attuned to their instincts and behave more instinctually. They may not deliberately reason out a problem in conscious terms as some humans do. But they are not automatons to be disposed of thoughtlessly. Even where their level of awareness may be very limited and controlled by instinct or genetics (ants come to mind, as well as more primitive species), animals remain intricate and responsive creations that deserve our respect and protection. All life is precious, however abundant and replaceable it may be in nature, and it is not ours to destroy except where necessary for our survival and well-being.[57]

In moral terms we must also beware of the purely anthropocentric argument for protecting wild species, often couched in ecological terms. In this view humans should be concerned about preserving other species, habitats, and ecosystems primarily because they are necessary for nature to function and thus for humans to survive. Again, the need for human survival and sustenance is indisputable. But in terms of human moral development this view of nature is inadequate and merely self-serving. We should care about protecting nature and its functioning also because we perceive that nature has value beyond us. This includes our value for other life forms, for the beauty of nature, and for the processes at work in nature. It is

---

55 As well as intelligence: in the higher levels of species (e.g., birds, mammals), it is being increasingly documented that animals can respond in an intelligent way even if they may not reason out a situation (and how many humans really do?). Certainly this is to be expected from evolutionary development—that intelligence and emotions evolved just as physical traits did—even though the human brain expanded disproportionately in terms of language and reasoning power.

56 A graphic example is provided by Aldo Leopold in his depiction of killing a wolf and "the fierce green fire dying in her eyes" (Aldo Leopold, *A Sand County Almanac* (New York: Oxford University Press, 1989), 130).

57 The same argument applies to plants, although it is not generally accepted that they have feelings or consciousness.

perfectly legitimate to care both about human survival in nature and about the survival of other species for their own sake, to be both a tree-hugger and a human-hugger.[58]

Even more inappropriate is the view advanced recently that endangered species and those that cannot adapt to human-induced changes in the environment do not deserve to survive by the laws of evolution. This argument is at once arrogant, heartless, and foolish, if only because it overlooks the real threat to human survival of losing other species. It also denies the significant differences between human-induced environmental change and most other environmental changes. Animal and plant species have evolved and adapted to natural changes, which are generally gradual on a regional or global scale (with the possible exception of large-scale meteor impact,[59] solar events, or widespread volcanic activity), although they may be sudden and catastrophic locally. The changes wrought by humans since the Industrial Revolution and recent population explosion are far more rapid. Human-induced climate change is the latest, and potentially most severe, of these changes. To expect other species to adapt to these unprecedented rates of change is to misapply evolutionary theory. It also reflects no concern for species other than our own.

Morality, Our World, and Ourselves

The moral perspective expounded here provides a framework by which to live our lives more sustainably. In this view there

---

58   It should not be necessary for a prominent contemporary geographer and author to declaim, as a way of asserting his position as "middle-of-the-road" between environmentalists and "non-environmentalists," that while he loves birds and other biota he loves his family and friends more and that his main interest in environmental issues is their effect on the human species, not on birds (Jared Diamond, *Collapse* (New York: Viking, 2005), 15-17).

59   This is thought to have caused the great extinction of the dinosaurs and other species at the end of the Cretaceous period.

are conceptually no bounds to the care and concern we should show toward the world around us, both animate and inanimate. This is not absolute, since our need to live in this world necessarily requires consumption of a portion of our environment. But the concepts of attitude and balance mitigate the effects of our takings and their apparent inconsistency with this perspective. We do not cease to value nature even as we consume part of it; and we ensure to the best of our knowledge that nature remains intact.

Real life presents myriad complexities in applying any theory or value system, and our moral relationship with nature is no exception. But its application would vastly improve the way we conduct both our commercial and our personal activities, and it would inevitably reverse the destructive direction our society is taking toward the environment and hence toward its own survival. As important, this moral perspective will allow us to be true to the best of human nature, to attain the highest character and behavioral ideals that we consider humane. Paradoxically, by being more human, we will also be more a part of nature. We will salvage our world as well as our souls.

CHAPTER 6

Now All Is Beautiful

....

I n morning on a lake up north the sun sparkles in a column on the water. The surface lies mostly calm for now, and the wind won't pick up until afternoon. With a faint, not unpleasant, whiff of gasoline from the motor boat, the image imprints on my young mind and returns happily whenever I see water shimmer by day. No matter that we get stranded in the middle when the engine dies, and Mom panics on shore as Dad futilely pulls the cord. Tranquility endures. Back on shore, brother and I play on the baby cliffs—he takes the high road, I take the low road; then we reverse.

Years later, as a teenager, I return to the northern lakes and every afternoon go down by the lake shore, amidst the white pines, to sit and stare at the waves lapping upon the rocks. The breeze blows my hair gently and turns pages on my book, which I hardly read. This is my summer retreat from the megalopolis I live in, the conglomeration of towns and cities within an hour of the Great City. I won't realize until years later my good fortune. I just know this feels so different from the world back home.

It is a confusing place in which to grow up. One town merges indistinguishably into another, with only the most subtle of changes in character; yet they are called different names. The nicer ones lie west and north on the ridge, commanding views of the plains and the skyline. Open space comes from golf courses, cemeteries, city parks, and lawns on corporate headquarters. Nature is found in the odd patch of woods as yet undeveloped and in reach of our bikes. The reservation on the ridge becomes a favorite haunt when I get my license to drive, but as a window-watcher in the back seat my nature preserve is mostly the Meadowlands I view quizzically as we drive to and from events in the Great City.

This Meadowlands, we've already seen, became one of many industrial pits of the megalopolis; yet it never quite forsook its native character. The rocky hill in the middle along which the turnpike runs gets chipped away over the years and painted with lovers' initials. But its igneous masses stand fast and continue to support a few trees. The filthy river continues to flow with water if not life, and common reed blankets the wetlands into the far distance amidst the roads and industrial parks. Nature, despoiled, blazes into my mind time and again on these trips to the Great City. I think of the summer world of sparkling water and lapping waves and wonder what has happened here. In my room of solitude back home I watch planes taking off into the western sun and envision a Hellenic world of harmony and beauty. My stage is set for outrage and action.

But not yet. I write my school mentor and wax ardently over a life to come of blissful creativity and mind above the fray. (Decades later he tells me he feared for my soul.) I leave the nest and climb the ivory tower of ever increasing abstraction, separation, and anomie. Our family dog is no longer my best friend, but a bother whose effusions I brush off my pants. Nature is reduced to the equations of chemistry and physics; living matter is ephemeral and counts for little. Science and literature studies culminate in . . . driving a taxi; then dabbling in music; then traveling abroad. I land a teaching job in the great East-West mountains overseas.

There I am arrested—by a beauty I had never known, by a transcendent presence that forever changes. Each morning as I awaken and look out my chalet window, then descend toward the school, the scene unfolds anew. My love for it deepens each day even as I marvel over the endless variety it presents. Some days are clear like a crystal, others nearly wrapped up in fog or low clouds filling the valley below. The leaden color of overcast does nothing to diminish its beauty, rather adds new tones and shades. The mountain opposite our village has the most pronounced changes in character, especially in times of alpenglow, while the distant peaks of the massif beyond the valley are always sublime. Only when we live in the clouds for days on end do spirits droop in everyone. Then all is white, still, motionless, and the scene becomes a memory we hope to be restored.

One year leads to the next, and I can see myself staying on and on, like many of my colleagues and expatriates. The beauty and loftiness are lulling, comforting . . . anesthetizing. I may never leave if I don't go now. I construct my future, and it is environmental, to protect this everywhere. I want to educate, but first must be educated. I return to the land whence I came.

Coming down to sea level deflates me at first. Cityscapes replace peaks, villages, and valleys. My studies and jobs bring me to favored places—woods, marshes, mountains—but only to visit. The rest of the time I am in small to large Eastern cities, charter members of the Rust Belt. This isn't quite the megalopolis I fled, but it isn't far off. And it seems so flat as to be almost claustrophobic.

Yet as I learn about the environment and how the natural world functions, my appreciation for it deepens. It is no longer merely a pretty picture or visual display, but an intricate conglomeration of interacting species, dynamic substrates, and nourishing media. All the visual dimensions by which I appreciate a "scene"—its form, balance, elegance, color, composition—are enriched by knowing what the plants are, how animals interact with it, and how the ecosystem operates and evolves. Artists may achieve this synthesis of intricate detail and overall subject within the limits of art alone. Knowledge brings me closer to the landscape, engaging my mind and senses in more ways, without sacrificing my appreciation of the big picture.

Moreover, something happens inside, and I begin to see everything as a continuum of nature or at least environment, some places more "built," others more "natural." Mount Vernon Square in Charm City, with its brownstones and cobblestones, is (I tell her who decries cities) exquisitely beautiful and comparable to many natural landscapes. Sun setting on buildings and skylines is urban alpenglow. Sky and clouds can always ravish our sights overhead, just as they beckoned me early on within suburbia. Plants and trees are most everywhere, even outside Frankl's concentration camp, where they gave hope to a dying woman.[60] I am no longer the ninth-grader who spoke before his class about the evils of the city. My friend and future spouse goes to the South to study architectural history, and the perspective is sealed.

I learn in the converse that nature is not all natural, that most landscapes and ecosystems bear marks of human use. Though discouraging at first, this too bridges the dichotomy of false purity and absolutes. The environment has been an admixture of humans and nature for a very long time. This opens up new opportunities for appreciation of beauty and knowledge. The same forces, the same values encompass the spectrum from wild to urban. They interact, as they always have, and thus humans remain truly part of the environment. While I rail at built environments that try to replace or ignore the natural, I realize they cannot ever do so. We are inextricably tied to our nature.

And that nature is irrevocably dual, all-encompassing, universal. I applaud and often seek the wilderness, the apparently untouched, and there should always be a place for the ends of the spectrum. More commonly we inhabit the mix, and we should cherish its every aspect. Intuitively I must have known this in my teenage years when I would eagerly bus to the Great City for its culture but also for its fabulous park, whose huge rock outcroppings loom up against a near background of skyscrapers. Schubert's *Great Symphony* with its plaintive opening horns and bathing strings and woodwinds made a perfect companion to

---

60 "Through that window she could see just one branch of a chestnut tree, and on the branch were two blossoms. 'I often talk to this tree,' she said to me. I was startled.... . Anxiously I asked her if the tree replied... . She answered, 'It said to me, "I am here–I am here–I am life, eternal life""" (Viktor E. Frankl, *Man's Search for Meaning* (New York: Pocket Books, 1984), 90).

the park and city. I felt no contradiction, and the world seemed all compact.

Much later that nature even came indoors as I became home to a beloved bird. His awakening and shutting down with the light (sun bird!) made me more mindful of the outside, and I watched in wonder as his brethren fared through blizzard and heat wave. I started going out just to see more of his kind, and one spring morning I came home with an aura of the tropics, from which many of them had just migrated. Now even my home harbored the spectrum. O Cary-bird!

We are inextricably tied to our nature, and it must reflect the full range of life and environment. We have the capacity to appreciate our world aesthetically, and we should use this more deeply and universally. While derelict built environments and degraded natural ones cannot truly be considered beautiful except in a limited pictorial way (if then), most everything else around us is worthy of our sight. Let our eyes dwell; we rarely look, much less see. (Young people, please look up from your digital toys!) All places have texture, variety, and endemic color. We don't have to travel to see the richness around us, and if we do it needn't be to iconic landmarks or attractions. Everywhere we go should provide an aesthetic adventure.

That same appreciation for the world around us deepens as we apply the moral perspective. In actuality, aesthetics and morality complement each other; they are different aspects of the same outlook. Integrity is just as important to aesthetics as to morality, as both respect the wholeness and functioning of the world around us. Individuals may be inclined more to one than to the other, but all of us can develop a sense for both, and should. These may be uniquely human attributes in perceiving the world around us, and we should foster them to realize our full potential. In so doing, we will solve the mind-body paradox and bring ourselves closer to the world. As all things are worthy of our care and concern, so all things are worthy of our perception and appreciation. All is indeed beautiful.

CHAPTER 7

Conclusion:
The Moral and Aesthetic Imperative

....

As a participant in greening the economy the past twenty years, I am both thrilled and discouraged by the progress we have made. This culture change, this revolution, has progressed from outright, almost ridiculous opposition by industry to becoming nearly mainstream. Yet the movement has not been able to turn around our society from its destructive and suicidal direction. The integration of sustainability into commerce remains far from complete, sometimes only like window dressing or at best very partial in its reach. Our everyday activities, as well as the prospect of bringing a burgeoning population in the developing world to our same material level, continue the downward spiral and burning of the environment on which we and all other species depend.

We have touched on many reasons for this inability to recognize and adequately resolve our environmental crisis even as our economy began to green. Decades of adversarial relationships in the United States among industry, government, and environmental advocacy groups[61] made difficult the transition to a more positive, cooperative partnership to address the many complex impacts of the economic life cycle. Industry sometimes aggravated the situation by digging in hard against the new paradigm with often specious arguments and well-funded groups they set up to sabotage third-party incentive programs.

In the 1990s and early 2000s the concept of clean production—evaluating and minimizing negative environmental and health impacts throughout the production life cycle—began to take hold over merely controlling pollution at the end of the process, and green standards for products and companies began to transform many markets. But the responsibility for driving green in the marketplace, for identifying the impacts and rooting them out with good alternatives, remained unclear. Practical issues like cost, product performance, and consumer demand for green tempered the enthusiasm of producers and purchasers alike. The depth of consumer commitment to sustainability continued to be questionable, as other concerns more mundane and material generally flooded out deeper ones. Moreover, everyone struggled to understand the technical aspects of sustainability issues in production and purchasing. Building green into the economy

---

61   Adversarial relationships among these parties may well have been necessary, at least in the US marketplace, in order to achieve the environmental progress that was made in the 1960s through 1980s. It did, however, have repercussions later. When environmental groups offered an olive branch to work with or even reward industry in the late 1980s and early 1990s, there was a great deal of suspicion and hard feeling to overcome on both sides. This was seen graphically in the slow uptake by industry of third-party environmental certification programs, which were considered a sure winner by the environmental community but a potential threat by industry.

became a new goal of the environmental movement, but how, by whom, and when remained unanswered.

We have seen that everyone participating in the economy bears responsibility for sustainability, although producers have a special responsibility because they are the initiators of the production cycle. This shared responsibility requires a new outlook and set of behaviors and a new definition of value and benefit in the economy and society. Increasingly corporations must consider sustainability an intrinsic dimension of their business, not an add-on or fad; recent legislation in several states to recognize "benefit" corporations that do just this is a hopeful development. On the other side, institutional purchasers must increasingly incorporate the broader measure of best value instead of lowest cost to guide what they buy. Retailers, the critical gateway to consumers, must in particular recognize their responsibility to consider the sustainability of the goods they offer consumers. The effort in recent years of some major retailers to work collectively to create environmental profiles of product categories and use them in their buying also shifts the economy in the right direction.

Consumers, ultimately the largest force in the economy, must be engaged to buy green. Considering the complexity of the issues, more sustainable products and services must be made available as the default choice for consumers, with individual taste and preference the only variables among sustainable choices. Given all the competing concerns in the marketplace, from basic needs to cost and status, consumers will only be able to lead the greening of the economy through the demand they exert on producers and retailers when they consciously become a part of the cultural revolution it entails.

A New Consciousness toward Our World

That consciousness will come about only through a conversion process that all of us must undertake. While informed by ecological science and environmental policy, the new consciousness is fundamentally based on a deeper morality and heightened aesthetic, with a new sensitivity to all that is around us. This approach will not only help us out of our current material, environmental, and spiritual crisis, but it can also improve how we conduct our lives and how we manage our society and its numerous problems.

Our moral scope—the circle of care and concern that we feel and act upon—must enlarge well beyond the traditional. To be truly moral beings who reflect the best in the human spirit, we must treat all others outside ourselves with the care we owe ourselves. Typically we act in our self-interest and for the benefit of groups we are part of or with which we identify. All else that lies outside this circle, whether human, animal, plant, or inanimate, receives scant attention or concern and may even be targeted for exploitation or destruction. While this self-centeredness may reflect a necessary aspect of life and survival and is certainly rampant throughout the animal kingdom, it does not truly represent the additional dimension of which humans are morally capable. To be the best human beings, we must treat all these others with comparable care and respect. In consuming the world around us, as we must for our own survival and well-being, we can apply this attitude as much as possible and use appropriate balance in weighing our needs against the needs of all others, so that we consider our impact on other peoples and countries as well as on other species and habitats.

This deeper moral perspective goes beyond the usual call for us to consider longer-term effects on our resource base or even our impact on future human generations. These essentially come back to considerations of survival—our own, in the first case, and our descendants', in the second. The new outlook certainly embraces these considerations, for moral concern and care originate in self-love and our innate self-centeredness as living beings.[62] But in its highest form human morality subsumes and transcends concern for the self and affinity groups and allows for comparable concern for all else.

Just as in early childhood we are sensitized to the needs of others, so in maturity we must show a new sensitivity toward all around us. In moral terms this involves extending our circle of care and concern. In aesthetic terms this means recognizing the beauty and integrity that is all around us. Aside from human poverty and environmental degradation, almost everything else that has retained its wholeness and functioning has an innate beauty to which we should be attuned. This heightened aesthetic complements the deeper morality by giving added value to the world around us and enhancing our desire to protect and treasure it.

With such an expanded, deepened sense of morality and aesthetics it will no longer be acceptable to have a disregard for nature or for others, broadly defined. Exploitation of nature, other human beings, and other species cannot be tolerated under this frame of mind. This is the new moral and aesthetic imperative we must embrace.

Aligning with a Changed World

Our world has changed drastically in the past few centuries; yet we continue to behave in more primitive ways, treating it as limitless

---

62 Arguably, our inability to achieve a deeper, broader morality hitherto (and our seemingly insane race to self-destruction) has stemmed from a lack of true self-value and self-respect, a kind of perpetual adolescence of our species.

and at the same time competing with each other to extract its wealth as quickly and completely as possible. We demonstrate the same tribalism as did our ancestors when living was indeed marginal and other groups of humans were necessarily a threat. This tribalism, transformed today into nationalism, must give way to a more global sense of ourselves and what needs to be protected and valued. Now we are one world more than ever before, a trend that will only grow over time through enhanced technologies of communication and transportation. Now, with environmental problems that are truly global in scope, we are all affected by degradation of the environment.

Our more unified but ever more finite world calls for a new outlook. We must convert ourselves to this outlook not just for the sake of human physical survival, although that is certainly at stake. It is also for the sake of us as truly human and humane beings. We must view cultural, ethnic, national, and religious differences not as threats but as enrichment. We must view other species not just as commodities we need to consume to survive, but also as fellow living creatures on this precious living planet. We must view "resources" not just as free wealth but as valued and limited treasures we must use wisely now and for the future. And we must view landscapes not just as convertible resources but as highly evolved habitats we are privileged to share with millions of other creatures.

But how?

How do we effect this conversion, this culture change, this fundamental and profound change in outlook to a deeper morality and aesthetics? How do we connect with the best that is human, treat each other and all of nature humanely, and embrace the moral and aesthetic imperative as we strive to create a green economy?

Or, in more mundane terms, what is an individual, and individual consumer, to do?

Overcoming Human Bias

Before tackling these questions and presenting a vision for the future, we must first address a troubling paradox. If human beings cannot yet demonstrate a sufficiently moral attitude toward themselves outside of identity or affinity groups (and often not even within them), how can we expect them to do so toward other species, much less inanimate nature? Can moral expansion happen in light of inhumane treatment of our own vulnerable groups, including children, less privileged classes and nations, and the like?

This contradiction between aspiration and reality hit home recently. Green Seal's standard for sustainable cleaning products was proposed by New York State to be applied under a 2005 state law for use in cleaning all its K-to-12 schools, public and private. Yet some groups complained, correctly, that our standard based its tests of toxicity on the accepted convention—the adult male. We had to revise the standard to ensure that it protected vulnerable populations such as children, the aged, and the infirm, and the state's mandate was thus fulfilled. So many aspects of our society are, in fact, similarly geared to the stronger elements of our population, with "safety nets" spun sporadically below to catch the more vulnerable. Indeed, examples of discrimination against more vulnerable, underprivileged classes and peoples (including children[63]) could fill volumes.

---

63 There is an additional paradox here, at least in the United States. While we increasingly coddle and over-protect our children in many ways (such as by being helicopter parents), we have ignored or inadequately addressed

The answer to this paradox is the moral imperative itself. We must change our moral values to encompass our own more vulnerable groups as well as others outside our identity or affinity groups. Recognizing the inadequacy of our current moral character as a society and the need to change is the essential step in creating a new morality that will address this paradox. Once we do so, the change in outlook will spark care not only for us collectively as humans, but also for the rest of the world around us. For, as we have shown, moral concern is not intrinsically bounded. Unhinging ourselves from primitive moral constraints and obligations can thus safely enable our moral expansion and liberate us to be more humane, both to other humans and to the rest of the living and inanimate world. The key in both cases is to make the transition to "others."

Let's see what such a world—morally and aesthetically enlarged—might look like.

A Green Platform and the Bethany Principles

More than twenty years ago, frustrated by the inability of the United States to address growing national and global environmental problems, I drafted a set of findings, principles, and actions ("A Green Platform") that could be the basis of a new green political party.[64] These are presented in their entirety in the appendix. On the adjoining page are the core principles ("The Bethany Principles," after the beach resort where they were conceived).

---

serious dangers to them in regard to junk food, alcohol, and toxins in the environment.

64   For good or for ill I did not actually found such a party.

The Bethany Principles

1. The biological needs of animals and plants will be given full consideration in human activities, both public and private, and will not necessarily be considered subordinate to human needs;

2. Destruction of other organisms and their habitats will be minimized and will be tolerated only when necessary for the survival or livelihood of humans or other species;

3. Destruction or modification of habitats will always require an equivalent restoration elsewhere, unless it is for the propagation of a threatened or endangered species;

4. Economics, including the cost of production and the price of products, must take into account the full effects of manufacturing on the environment and the true cost of depletion of natural resources;

5. Government and society at large must give highest priority to preserving biological diversity, restoring environmental quality, eliminating ecologically destructive activities and modes of consumption, and stabilizing global climate;

6. The United States must take a leadership role at two levels: first of all, by ensuring that it applies these principles in its own activities and does nothing to encourage their violation abroad; second, by working vigorously to get the community of nations to adopt these principles and by actively leading other nations in programs to preserve biological diversity, environmental quality, and the bioclimatic regime;

7. A new appreciation and value for biological diversity and ecological quality must be instilled at all levels of society and through all educational means, not in an authoritarian

way, but rationally and through the joy of discovery and wonder;

8. This new ethic will serve to guide public and private activities, rather than a host of new regulations and bureaucratic devices such as environmental impact statements;

9. Congress shall nevertheless pass, and agencies shall faithfully implement, laws with these governing principles.

10.)
)
11.)   [see text]
)
12.)

These principles reflect my purely environmental anguish and hopes at that time, so they omit consideration of the human victims of our more primitive morality. Clearly equity and justice toward other humans should be added. Environmental justice is a way of looking at our economic activities and environmental programs in terms of the classes of people actually affected by them. Where do we site hazardous waste and industrial plants? Whom do we protect with our environmental laws, and what environmental concerns do we even consider worth addressing? Beyond even these, we must consider the effects of our society's activities on the economic status of various peoples, both in our country and around the world. Who benefits economically, and who gets less than their fair share of what they produce? Fair trade programs strive to give full value to farmers in developing countries for their commodity crops. More broadly, the continuing controversy over outsourcing jobs to the developing world concerns both the loss of jobs in developed countries and the potential exploitation of workers in developing ones.

Moreover, if these principles were written today, they would include another dimension that relates to much of this book, the green economy. For instance, outsourcing to the developing world has significant ramifications for the environment in addition to potential exploitation of workers overseas. The concept of cleaner production and the responsibility of producers, retailers, institutional purchasers, and consumers to consider environmental, health, and social impacts, as explored in earlier chapters, demand their own principles. These would complement the economic principle for full cost accounting and impact assessment by calling for more sustainable practices and materials throughout the economic system.

So let us add the following three principles to bring the Bethany Principles more up-to-date:

10. Equity and justice toward all human beings must govern all economic and social activities.

11. Considerations of long-term sustainability will be included in all economic activities, including resource extraction, selection of materials, manufacturing operations and practices, and product life-cycle management.

12. All parties in the supply chain and economic system bear responsibility for considering these principles in their activities—especially producers, but also retailers, institutional purchasers, consumers, and all users of products and services.

The Bethany Principles are clearly aspirational; yet they illustrate the kind of thinking we must begin to adopt in order to live with ourselves and others in this world. The emphasis of these principles is on protection of other species, habitats, and biological diversity because their destruction is the most irreversible and long-term of the changes we are causing to the environment. Species take millions of years to evolve, habitats hundreds. Climate change will affect both severely, and certain aspects of climate change itself may be irreversible, at least on a scale of centuries. We cannot (and should not try to!) remake species that we cause to go extinct. Moreover, it is toward other species, our very own brethren on this living planet, that the moral imperative speaks most pointedly and poignantly. Consideration of the needs of other living beings—and, yes, for many animal species, consideration of their sensations and even feelings—must be part of our new consciousness.

The moral imperative is encapsulated in the very first two principles, supplemented by the tenth just added. The first principle puts almost on par ("not necessarily. . . subordinate") the needs of other organisms and our own. This is a bold statement and might seem unrealistic if it were not immediately qualified—and actually expanded—by the second principle, which states that consumption of other species and their habitats by humans will be limited to what humans need for survival and livelihood. We might want to add, as we did earlier, the human need for well-being, recognizing that this requires qualification in terms of what is sustainable. That is the subject for another book, delineating a reasonable but sustainable lifestyle. If the moral imperative is accepted and these principles followed, we have a much better chance of finding the right balance of everyone's needs and saving our world for ourselves and all other living things in the process.

The Green Platform goes on to list an agenda for change that includes a number of more specific but still broad and ambitious goals relating to energy, waste, greenhouse gas emissions, and habitat preservation. It then states that, effective immediately, all residential and industrial development shall take place only on lands currently used for these purposes, and there shall be a universal policy of no net loss of habitat or biota. These are certainly idealistic and perhaps even extreme goals, as population grows and people seek more space and goods for a more affluent lifestyle. But this situation will without doubt become reality sometime in the future. At some point, if we continue in the current mode, we will run out of developable land on the earth. These goals, therefore, call on us to consider the land, habitat, and species we are consuming and make plans to reduce our takings to allow the earth's ecosystems to exist sustainably into the future.

While idealistic, the Green Platform (supplemented as discussed) provides us with goals and a direction to follow, consistent with the moral and aesthetic imperative. These can inform our plans and actions as we struggle to create a more sustainable economy and world. Certainly we face great challenges here. We must provide adequate material support and well-being to those in the developing world and overcome extreme economic disparity everywhere while making our economic system sustainable. This seems almost an impossible task—to create more out of less when we are already so constrained in terms of the earth's resources, carrying capacity, and climate.

Fundamental Change Is Required

The Green Platform and this book do not attempt to present a detailed roadmap with specific actions to achieve sustainability under these moral, aesthetic, and ecologically limiting terms. Other environmental writers have capably laid out global action plans and policies for dealing with our environmental crisis.[65] It will take a combination of new laws, new technologies, new behaviors, and a new outlook to effect the change we desperately need to avert ecological crisis and provide for the well-being of the world's growing population. The key message here is that the latter—a new outlook—is what we need most now, because nothing else has yet sufficed to alter society's direction.

Just as prescriptions to solve our environmental crisis have been offered at the macroeconomic and policy level, so too have various books provided guidelines to consumers on how to buy and behave more sustainably.[66] We need not duplicate these here. Many of the guidelines are helpful, practical, and on point, and if everyone followed them we would be on the road to a more sustainable economy and world. We would still have to deal with the mess we have already created, including the excessive load of

---

65 For example, James Gustave Speth, *America the Possible: Manifesto for a New Economy, 2012,* and *The Bridge at the Edge of the World,* 2008; Lester Brown, *World on the Edge,* 2011; Paul Hawken et al., *Natural Capitalism,* 1999.

66 For example, Ed Begley Jr., *Living Like Ed: A Guide to the Eco-Friendly Life,* 2008, and *Ed Begley Jr.'s Guide to Sustainable Living: Learning to Conserve Resources and Manage an Eco-Conscious Life,* 2009; Diane MacEachern, *Big Green Purse: Use Your Spending Power to Create a Cleaner, Greener World,* 2008; Diane Gow McDilda, *365 Ways to Live Green: Your Everyday Guide to Saving the Environment,* 2008; Elizabeth Rogers, Thomas M. Kostigen, *The Green Book: The Everyday Guide to Saving the Planet One Simple Step at a Time,* 2007; Greg Horn, *Living Green: A Practical Guide to Simple Sustainability,* 2006; Crissy Trask, *It's Easy Being Green: A Handbook for Earth-Friendly Living,* 2006; Michael Brower, Warren Leon, *The Consumer's Guide to Effective Environmental Choices: Practical Advice from the Union of Concerned Scientists,* 1999.

greenhouse gases in the atmosphere, the continuing loss of vital habitats and the thousands or millions of species that perish with them, and the dispersal of toxins throughout the environment. And we would still have to devise a more sustainable framework for societal development, particularly as relates to use of land, resources, and materials or chemicals. If consumers were to become a force for sustainability, however, much of the impetus for exploitation would halt or reverse.

But, in fact, neither policy solutions nor consumer guidelines for a more sustainable world are being followed. We noted earlier that the "green" consumer is a miniscule slice of the pool. While we know generally what we have to do, both at the societal and the individual level, we are not doing it, or we are doing it too slowly and partially and inadequately. This failure derives from a value system that is still incapable of dealing with our environmental and existential crisis and that has, in fact, been the cause of it. We need a basic change in our human values to relate properly to our world and to ourselves, and so to salvage all of it from our continuing despoliation.

Those of us in the environmental movement have long agonized over our inability to genuinely move the economy and society to a more sustainable direction. We have failed to persuade the majority of Americans to change their ways by information, guilt, regulation, policy, or even voluntary programs. In one fell swoop nature (in the form of events such as Hurricanes Katrina and Sandy) does a better job of waking us all up, but then we go back to building on beaches and buying SUVs. Environmentalists have avoided the values approach as too esoteric, elitist, or time-consuming; yet we keep on butting against it. My organization from its very start declared that a company's motives were inconsequential as long as it did the right thing (that is, made its products or services more sustainable to meet Green Seal standards). While we have transformed markets this way, we have not yet transformed the economy or motivated consumers to do so. Until all of us confront the fundamentals, the underlying human values, our society will not achieve sustainability.

Technology and the Imperative

Many people, including me at times, put much hope in technology and human ingenuity to save us from our environmental predicament. Certainly, technology and human ingenuity can—and may have to—provide solutions to some specific problems, if guided by the moral perspective and balance espoused here.

For example, in the short term, technology may be the only solution to ruinous climate change. Since our economies are still heavily dependent on conventional fossil fuels, the conversion to renewable energy sources will likely take decades unless we find a breakthrough energy source that is both carbon-neutral and sustainable in terms of environmental and social impacts as well as supply. Moreover, we must engineer a way to remove much of the excess carbon dioxide and other global-warming gases we have put into the atmosphere in the past two centuries in order to stabilize our already vacillating global climate.

Individuals and small groups are currently working on this energy and climate problem, but what is needed is a society-wide effort to find a fix for climate change, especially because actions on the policy and political fronts have been so hampered and lame. As momentous and complex as anthropogenic climate change is, its cause derives from basic physics and chemistry, and we should be able to devise counteractions while we render our energy systems more sustainable. Nor should we just prepare to "adapt" to climate change; this may turn out to be a foolish hope, and it certainly does not help all of the other species on our planet which cannot readily do so (imagine what kind of an ark we would have to build).

Yet technology and ingenuity alone cannot rescue us. They will not bring back habitats or species, as much as we pretend that we can "restore" ecosystems. They will not make development and resource extraction sustainable, although they may help mitigate their impacts. More likely, technology will devise new, more powerful ways to extract wealth from the earth, as we are currently seeing with hydraulic fracturing for gas and oil, where environmental protection is racing to keep up with the action. New technologies will also continually confront us with challenging moral issues, as in the development and use of genetically modified organisms (GMOs).[67] Other global environmental issues such as pervasive toxic pollution may be helped by technology, as in the greening of the economy, which removes harmful ingredients through better chemical and process technologies. But in all these instances the impetus behind technology must be guided by the moral imperative, lest the technology merely worsen our overall condition.

In sum, appropriate societal development will be vastly facilitated by realigning society's priorities in accordance with

---

67   GMOs are indeed troubling from the perspective of the moral and aesthetic imperative. Invading a species' chromosomes and then splicing in a foreign gene could well qualify as the archetypical act of destroying an organism's integrity. Breeding to strengthen certain innate characteristics or even mutations at least maintains intact the genetics of the species. The issue gets problematic, however, when GMOs can be presented as highly beneficial to human health (e.g., disease prevention) or welfare (e.g., food supply), assuming potential environmental issues can be addressed. In such cases the alleged benefit must be weighed against the "taking," keeping the principles of attitude (care, respect) and balance in mind. This suggests that discrete, focused, *careful* uses of GMOs might be appropriate, but wholesale development of GMOs for profit would not be.

the moral and aesthetic imperative. We need to come into general agreement on the human values we should hold toward ourselves and toward the rest of the world—that the circle of care is generally boundless and only limited by practical necessities of survival and well-being. Then we will seek to bring our impoverished peoples and classes out of poverty and oppression, and we will always consider the fate of other species and their habitats as we take care of ourselves.

Some Ways to Start: Peace and the Power of Two

The first step in making change is to recognize the need for change. The next step is to identify what needs to change and to what new state. The discussion so far has strived to fulfill these first two steps. The subsequent step, the current question, is how to convince humans to change accordingly. Of course, this is an age-old question. All religions, philosophies, and value systems present themselves as the truth and the right way to live, and they attempt to convince everyone to follow their way. I, too, am offering a way I believe will solve our environmental crisis and many of our social and individual ills. I realize it is idealistic, the ultimate morality, but I believe the time has come to embrace it.

I have no magical answer for how. But here are a few ideas for both how and how not to instill the moral and aesthetic imperative throughout human society.

One obvious way to start in this direction is for the civilized world to reduce armaments and to forbear waging war. Imagine the resources that would be freed, the talents that would be redirected, and the human potential that would be saved. If this work is a call for us to reach deep into ourselves to connect with the best that is human, might we not ask ourselves finally—finally—to act as adults in a world that has far transcended the tribal, marginal conditions that made our ancestors fight constantly among themselves? Can we not expect that we will treat each other humanely and with care, not look for more efficient ways to kill each other? Disparities in living conditions and inequities in society can create unrest and conflict, but it is not typically these that have driven us to war in the past hundred years (the truly downtrodden rarely rise up). Since we all face the predicament of environmental limits and degradation, we must work together as one people to solve the problem of sustainable development. For surely, if we do not, environmental deterioration will only intensify the potential for conflict among peoples and nations as well as threaten our very survival.

As for what we can all do as individuals, we have heard of the power of one: the individual—like the brave soul who stood in front of a tank on Tiananmen Square, or Rosa Parks, who refused to give up her seat to a white person—who can galvanize the world by his or her actions and even start a movement for social change. We need the power of us all in the new world of sustainability. For society truly to change, as many people as possible must enlarge their circle of care as the basis for the new morality.

We have new tools today to propagate ideas widely throughout the world, namely, the Internet and social media. When the Internet first emerged on a wide-scale basis in the 1990s, many of us were euphoric that finally there was a connector in our world that would transcend artificial national and demographic boundaries and unite people to meet global challenges. That promise was set back abruptly by the terrorist attacks of September 2001 and subsequent events, but it remains and has grown in potential through the emergence in the 2000s of social media. We parents complain about social media and our children's addiction to it. Imagine if social media could be harnessed to create new values and effect social change.

I propose the Power of Two, driven potentially through social media. Recall the way numbers increase enormously through exponential growth: 1, 2, 4, 8, 16, 32, 64, 128, 256, 512, 1024, 2048, 4096, 8192, 16384, etc. This series is simply two multiplied by itself each time, or 2^n, where n = 0, 1, 2, 3, 4, 5. . . . If each person who embraced the moral and aesthetic imperative were to gently convince or enlist *two* other people to this view through direct contact or social media, we could cover the United States (around 315 million) in about twenty-eight doublings. In other words, assuming each person reaches two others, we would have to do this only twenty-eight times to reach all Americans. Globally, at 7.06 billion, we would need thirty-three doublings, or only five more doublings than for the United States alone! (Note how quickly exponentials grow from millions to billions.)

Social media can provide the means to achieve this massive scale of communication and conversion. In the traditional social framework an individual would typically count his or her network in the dozens or scores, at most. These included family, relatives, friends, colleagues, and acquaintances—all maintained by direct contact or by telephone and letter. Today, through smart phones and similar devices that link directly to the Internet and many social network Web sites, an individual may easily have an active network of several hundred other people with whom they are "connected" and can communicate.

Now these vastly enlarged individual networks through social media are largely used for light social intercourse and entertainment. Typically the younger generation, the predominant users of social media, obtains enjoyable news (such as new trends), shares opinions and life events or TV shows, and tracks celebrities and thought leaders through these connections.[68] These are all good. But imagine again if these vast networks were, in addition, employed to communicate about deeper values and about specific social and environmental situations where the moral and aesthetic imperative could come into play. Social media has already been used in such a way to foment social unrest and even revolutions in the Middle East and the United States (e.g., the Occupy Movement), as well as to exert consumer pressure on corporations, so its power to galvanize and organize people to effect change is not just theoretical. If our younger people were to dedicate a portion of their social media time to important environmental and social issues domestically and globally, they could use social media to shape these events according to the moral and aesthetic imperative.

An individual can learn about an important environmental or social issue in the United States or around the world and communicate to his or her social network how the moral and aesthetic imperative might be applied in resolving the issue. After an appropriate discussion among interested network members they could agree on a position on the issue and how to move it forward. Using the Power of Two, they could propagate these ideas to others in their own networks, who could pick it up in a similar vein. Even if just a few people out of each network of several hundred really take an issue to heart, the Power of Two suggests that their commitment and activism can multiply quickly around the globe through the connectedness of networks and exponential expansion.

---

68   Brielle Welzer (Green Seal's expert in social media), personal communication.

About the only danger I see in using this tool is the possibility of issue proliferation and fatigue. Individuals may be bombarded from many people about many different issues of concern. But part of the networking process through social media can be to coalesce efforts behind a limited number of priority environmental and social issues, such as climate change, habitat loss, greener production, poverty, war, and political oppression. Moreover, our social media generation has become rather adept at multi-tasking among many different topics; here is a place for them to apply this skill for the greater good of the world.

Social media can also lead by example and positive peer reinforcement. Techniques like gamification are being applied in business and in sustainability programs leveraging people's innate desire to do well and keep up with their peers. While the moral and aesthetic imperative concerns our innermost values, it could incorporate gamified techniques such as goals and virtual rewards to encourage people to enlarge their circle of care and commitment to the principles. I would certainly not want to see it trivialized, and any such approach must still focus on core values. The point is rather that the moral and aesthetic imperative is about positive values and feelings, about expanding the scope of our care, appreciation, and love to everything in the world around us. So any movement or method to propagate it must be consistent with this purpose and character, and anything that enhances the joy and wonder of the experience will more likely lead to its acceptance.

I hasten to add what this effort should not involve: dogma, ideology, coercion, force, shame, ridicule, guilt, hurt, pain, punishment. Human history is rife with instances of good thoughts gone bad, often by those who proselytize a leader's idea. If this is a crusade, as it must be to some degree to save the world, it will be conducted with all the humanity and humaneness that form its core principles.

And then the world will burn no more, and the fires will stay deep down and high in the sky, as plants, animals, and people return under the Light.

The world will burn no more (the fires stay deep and high) as the circle opens on people's view of their world.

The world burns no more (the fires stay deep and high) as we finally love one another as ourselves.

The world burns no more (the fires stay deep and high) as we love our fellow creatures and the land for themselves.

And the world burns no more (the fires stay deep and high) as we become what we always wanted to be.

A Green Platform

We find that:

1. Destruction of habitat and impairment of valuable ecosystems continues unabated and in many cases is accelerating;

2. Elimination of plant and animal species and disruption of the global climate represent the two biggest threats to life on earth as we know it and if unchecked will fundamentally undermine biological and human life systems;

3. The attention and resources devoted to solving environmental and ecological problems caused by humans are wholly inadequate, considering the

significance of these problems both to humans and to all life on earth;

4. Conventional approaches to solving these problems in the governmental and economic arena are not sufficient and will merely prolong the destruction and heighten the eventual crises toward which our present behavior leads us;

5. The major political parties fail to recognize the gravity of environmental problems, treating them as another on a long list of agenda items, interchangeable according to political trends and tastes;

6. A new political philosophy and social ethic are needed, in order to salvage the diversity of life, ensure the survival of humans, and instill in humans a deep appreciation for the richness of other life on earth.

We hold to the following principles [the Bethany Principles]:

1. The biological needs of animals and plants will be given full consideration in human activities, both public and private, and will not necessarily be considered subordinate to human needs;

2. Destruction of other organisms and their habitats will be minimized and will be tolerated only when necessary for the survival or livelihood of humans or other species;

3. Destruction or modification of habitats will always require an equivalent restoration elsewhere, unless it is for the propagation of a threatened or endangered species;

4. Economics, including the cost of production and the price of products, must take into account the full effects of manufacturing on the environment and the true cost of depletion of natural resources;

5. Government and society at large must give highest priority to preserving biological diversity, restoring environmental quality, eliminating ecologically destructive activities and modes of consumption, and stabilizing global climate;

6. The United States must take a leadership role at two levels: first of all, by ensuring that it applies these principles in its own activities and does nothing to encourage their violation abroad; second, by working vigorously to get the community of nations to adopt these principles, and by actively leading other nations in programs to preserve biological diversity, environmental quality, and the bioclimatic regime;

7. A new appreciation and value for biological diversity and ecological quality must be instilled at all levels of society and through all educational means, not in an authoritarian way, but rationally and through the joy of discovery and wonder;

8. This new ethic will serve to guide public and private activities, rather than a host of new regulations and bureaucratic devices such as environmental impact statements;

9. Congress shall nevertheless pass, and agencies shall faithfully implement, laws with these governing principles.

We propose the following agenda:

By the year …,[69] the United States of America shall:

1. Use non-polluting renewable energy sources or fail-safe, non-polluting nuclear energy sources for all major industrial, domestic, and transportation needs;
2. Reduce by ninety-nine percent or more the hazardous and non-hazardous waste produced in industries, homes, and municipalities, through waste minimization and recycling;
3. Develop safe technologies for and, in conjunction with other nations, achieve the reduction or neutralization of excess greenhouse gases to 1960 levels so as to stabilize global climate;
4. Dedicate for preservation and protection in perpetuity a significant percentage of its territorial area for the purpose of preserving and enhancing biological and ecological diversity and providing wildlife refuges.

Effective immediately, the United States of America shall:

5. Cease further industrial and residential development of lands not currently used for these purposes, concentrating such uses on lands currently devoted to these uses;
6. Adopt a universal policy of no net loss of habitat or biota, unless required for the preservation of an endangered or threatened species;

---

69 When this was originally composed, ca. 1989, I put the year 2000 here. The reader is invited to predict when these goals might actually be met.

7. Work with other nations and international organizations and provide leadership to abate global environmental threats, including destruction of species, loss of habitat (particularly tropical and temperate rainforest), and climate change due to increased greenhouse gases.

About the Author

....

 Arthur B. Weissman, Ph.D. is an environmental professional with over thirty years of experience. As president and CEO of Green Seal, he has led the organization both as a force to promote the green economy and as the premier non-profit certifier of green products and services in the United States. He has also worked for the US Environmental Protection Agency, US Congress, and The Nature Conservancy and has degrees from Johns Hopkins University, Yale University, and Harvard College. His other interests include family, classical music and piano, hiking, birding, reading, and writing.

CPSIA information can be obtained at www.ICGtesting.com
Printed in the USA
LVOW03*2340080514

384966LV00012BC/278/P